Prism and Ken

Terry Johnson's work as a playwright includes a version of Edward Ravenscroft's *The London Cuckolds*, *Dead Funny* and *Hysteria*. He is the recipient of major British theatre awards including Playwright of the Year 1995; Critics' Circle Best New Play 1995; Writers' Guild Best West End Play 1995; Olivier Award Best Comedy 1994; the Meyer-Whitworth Award 1993; and the John Whiting Award 1991. He also won the 2010 Tony Award for Best Director of a Musical for his production of *La Cage aux Folles*. His play *Piano/Forte* premiered at the Royal Court Jerwood Theatre Downstairs in 2006 and, most recently, his play *Ken* premiered at Hampstead Theatre Downstairs in April 2016.

T0353526

Terry Johnson

Prism and Ken

Bloomsbury Methuen Drama
An imprint of Bloomsbury Publishing Plc

B L O O M S B U R Y
LONDON • OXFORD • NEW YORK • NEW DELHI • SYDNEY

Bloomsbury Methuen Drama

An imprint of Bloomsbury Publishing Plc

50 Bedford Square   1385 Broadway
London   New York
WC1B 3DP   NY 10018
UK   USA

www.bloomsbury.com

**BLOOMSBURY, METHUEN DRAMA and the Diana logo
are registered trademark of Bloomsbury Publishing Plc**

First published 2017

© Terry Johnson, 2016

British Library Cataloguing-in-Publication Data
A catalogue record for this book is available from the British Library

ISBN: PB: 978-1-3500-5691-6
ePDF: 978-1-3500-5693-0
ePub: 978-1-3500-5694-7

Library of Congress Cataloging-in-Publication Data
A catalog record for this book is available from the Library of Congress

Series: Modern Plays

Cover image © Shaun Webb

Typeset by Country Setting, Kingsdown, Kent CT14 8ES

To find out more about our authors and books visit www.bloomsbury.com.
Here you will find extracts, author interviews, details of forthcoming events
and the option to sign up for our newsletters.

Prism

Prism was first staged at Hampstead Theatre, London, on 6 September 2017, with the following cast:

Jack   Robert Lindsay
Nicola/Katie   Claire Skinner
Lucy/Betty/Marilyn   Rebecca Night
Mason/Bogie/Miller   Barnaby Kay

Writer and Director   Terry Johnson
Designer   Tim Shortall
Lighting Designer   Ben Ormerod
Sound Designer   John Leonard
Composer   Colin Towns
Video Designer   Ian William Galloway
Casting Directors   Suzanne Crowley and Gilly Poole

Characters

Jack
Nicola/Katie
Lucy/Betty/Marilyn
Mason/Bogie/Miller

Note

Prism is a fiction, loosely based on the extraordinary life of Jack Cardiff.

Artistic licence has been taken, as have a great many liberties.

Act One

Scene One

A large double garage in the village of Denham, which has been renovated into a small museum. An up-and-over door to the back and a skimpy wooden door to the side.

It is a pleasant place to be. It has an elegant chaise, a comfortable old sofa and a nice armchair. It has a large desk and swivel chair. It is filled to the rafters with memorabilia, barely any of which we can see right now, as the room is in virtual darkness. Film-making equipment. Lights, director's chairs, film cameras and stills cameras.

A Technicolor camera – a magnificent blue/green and chrome original.

Bits of props and costume. Movie posters. Objects recognisable from movies. A wonderland derived from A Matter of Life and Death, The Red Shoes, Black Narcissus, The Prince and the Showgirl, The African Queen. *Prominent on one wall, and lifted by some ambient light through a tiny window at the back, are six large black-and-white studio portraits of movie stars, including Audrey Hepburn, Marilyn Monroe, Katharine Hepburn, Marlene Dietrich and Sophia Loren. The posters and the pictures have their own luminescence which will alter to illuminate the action of the play. We hear voices off.*

Jack (*off*)   Wherever I'm going I don't want to go.

Mason (*off*)   That one there.

Jack (*off*)   Wherever you think you're taking me, unless it's the pub.

Mason (*off*)   The other one.

Jack (*off*)   Is it the pub?

Mason (*off*)   It's the other one. Next to your thumb.

Jack (*off*)   I don't much like the other pub.

Mason (*off*)   The other *button*. Press it.

A mechanical clonk and the self-raising door begins to open on to bright sunlight. It reveals foreground a good pair of deck shoes and Jermyn Street slacks. Further upstage a pair of brogues and corduroy trousers. Further upstage still, black ankle-boots and leggings. The door stops a few feet up, creating a shallow rectangular vista of the lane beyond.

Jack   Ahah!

Mason   Keep pressing.

Jack   Polyvision.

Mason   Keep it pressed.

Jack   Only used the once. Needed three projectors. Barnum and Bailey nonsense. Only fit for Disneyland. We're not in fucking Mousewitz, are we?

Mason   No. Push with your thumb.

The door jerks eight inches.

Jack   That's better. Panavision Super wide 70 mil! Aspect ratio 2.76 to one.

Mason   Press the bloody button.

Jack *operates the door again, stops it again.*

Jack   Now here's a novelty. Cinerama! 2.59 to one. Three projectors, three cameras, so they had to cheat their bloody eyelines. This would be you, this would be me. She'd be out of focus. I'd be talking to the − red thing for letters.

Mason   Pillar box.

Jack   I'd be talking to the pillar box.

Mason   So what's new?

Jack   *How the West Was Won*. Bit of a winner. Brothers Grimm. Grim indeed. Filed for bankruptcy. 'We can't afford ourselves, but This Is Cinerama!' Bloody clowns. That trailer ran for ten years, though; credit where it's due. Who *is* that?

Mason   Press the button.

Jack *operates the door, stops it again.*

Jack   Back in the day they used to slide sideways!

Mason   Sideways?

Jack   We're going to need a bigger sound stage than this.

He sits down, cross-legged, on the drive. Late sixties, cashmere sweater or smart blazer. Jaunty hat.

Mason   Don't sit there; the paving's damp.

Jack   You see, now we're talking. Cinemascope! 2.35 to one. Thirty-five-mil stock, but the image squished. Very ingenious, *very* grainy. Image quality was always going to be compromised unless they went 70 mil.

Mason   Get up, for Christ's sake.

Jack   I could run you through Superscope, Technirama, Cinemiracle, Vistarama but they're much of a muchness until . . .

He operates the door, stops it.

Todd AO. Super Panavision. 2.20 to one. Unassailable winners of the widescreen skirmish.

Mason   It's a garage door.

Jack   I won't be able to shoot with anything wider than a fifty in a place that size.

Mason   Just get up and go through it.

Jack *operates the door, revealing himself and also* **Mason***, mid-forties. And further up the drive,* **Lucy***, mid-twenties, smart but reserved. A nose piercing.*

Jack   1.77; the curse of fucking television. Talk about going backwards.

He stops the door, entranced by the current ratio.

Now look. Look at that. Both of you, whoever she is . . . Academy ratio. 1.37 to one. Perfection. Yet totally random; 1.37. Why? Because – the round blue thing – water and land –

Mason   The world?

Jack   The world – was no longer silent. They had to make room down the side for the noise. Irrational and arbitrary, but beautiful; Academy ratio.

Mason *enters the garage.*

Mason   Come inside. Tell me what you think.

Jack   No, no; last but by no means least . . .

He operates the door, it stops at its limit.

Where it all began; Three by four. One to 1.33 recurring. Our simple but silent past.

Mason   *Your* past. Why don't you step into it?

Jack   Because I might never get back, old son.

Mason   Please; just come inside.

Jack *steps inside.* **Lucy** *stays at a distance, watching.*

Jack   Call this a sound stage? It's the size of a bloody garage.

Mason   It *is* the garage.

Jack   Is it? Then what's all this bloody stuff? Where's the . . . thing?

Mason   The what?

Jack   The thing you with your feet. And turn the wheel. The car! Where's the bloody car?

Mason   It's parked opposite the pub.

Jack   Splendid. Mine's a scotch and soda.

Mason   You're not in the pub. You're in the garage.

Jack (*astonished*)   Am I?

Mason   Yes.

Jack   Then where's the car?

Mason   It's up the road.

Jack   I don't like the . . . thing with wings. Big Lizard. Dragon! The George! I'll have a drink here.

Mason   This isn't the pub. It's the garage.

Jack   Is it?

Mason   Yes.

Jack   Where's the car, then? I thought you said we'd meet in the pub.

Mason   That was last week, for Christ's sake.

Jack   Where the bloody hell have you taken me this time? The point of a location, Mason, is you have to be able to *shoot* in it! There's no height in here. Hang on; you can't fool me. We're under the stage. Where's the Wurlitzer?

Mason   The what?

Jack   Dad said I could go up on it. Look at this, Dad. Time step!

He tap-dances.

Anything Dad can do. Shuffle-ball-change. Eh?

Mason   Very clever, but your dad's not here.

Jack   He promised me we'd go under the stage and up on the Wurlitzer. He's in his dressing room. I saw a chorus girl weeing in the sink. I saw a man in er – penguin. In a hat.

Mason   Evening dress?

Jack   Top hat and tails; murmuring to that chorus girl. 'Not even if I gave you this gold watch?' Buffaloes, I want to show Dad.

Mason   How old are you, Jack?

Jack   Not as young as I was.

Mason   You're older than your dad was when he died.

Jack   Am I? No.

A tap flourish, but a tired one.

Getting on a bit, I grant you. If I keep practising, Dad's gonna put me in the act.

Mason   He never did, though. In his eyes, you were never good enough.

Jack   You think so?

Mason   I know so.

Jack   Standing in the wings, though, watching him. And watching Mum. Dazzled by the side-light. I bend my neck to get her head between the light and my eyes. Suddenly she's rim-lit, radiant.

Mason   They died twenty years ago, Dad. You're not in the wings; you're in the garage.

Jack (*astonished*)   Am I?

Mason   Would you please just . . . look around you.

Jack *looks around him. There is nothing casual about the way he looks. He looks more intently than other men.*

Jack   Good Lord.

Mason   Now do you see?

Jack   Of course I see . . .

Mason   You see where you are?

Jack   Yes. I see. (*To* **Lucy**.) Hello.

Lucy   Hello.

Mason   And?

Jack   Ha!

Mason   Well?

Jack   Well what?

Mason   What do you think?

Jack   I think this is bloody strange. It's as if I'm in my head.

Mason   Which is increasingly debatable.

Jack   Have I shrunk or did my head get bigger?

Mason   Neither; keep calm.

Jack   That was a joke, you numpty. What is this bloody stuff? Where the FUCK AM I?

Mason   You're in the garage!

Jack   I don't need any clues from you!

Mason   Look around you.

Jack   Perfectly capable, thank you.

Mason (*to* **Lucy**)   You see?

Lucy   Yes.

Mason   We're not at our wits' end.

Lucy   No.

Jack   Mine's a martini.

Mason   It's just the end of our wits are in plain sight.

Jack   I want it dirty.

Mason   Mine closer than his, frankly.

Lucy   Yes.

Jack   We're in the garage.

Mason   Are you pleasantly surprised, at least?

Jack   Oh, yes. Persistently surprised. Relentlessly, in fact.

Mason   It's a place you can . . .

Jack   What? Where?

Mason   . . . remember things.

Jack *uncovers and recognises the Technicolor camera.*

Jack   Ah. This I remember.

Mason   Good. So you should.

Jack   Been on the edge of, er – when you bash a boiled egg – when a mountain's on fire!

Mason   A volcano.

Jack   Edge of a volcano with this sweetheart. In deserts, jungles. Over the Coliseum in that – plane with bombs in it – bomber plane! Doh. Seen some sights, she and I. Failed her MOT, though. You can't get the parts. Did me proud. Used to get ninety out of her on the way to Shepperton – (*Singing* The Avengers *theme tune.*) Bom bom bom, bom bom bom, bom bom bom. Good God. Is that a Vermeer?

Mason   No, that's yours.

Jack   I own a Vermeer?

Mason   You painted it.

Jack   No, no, no, no. I'm Jack.

Mason   Yes, you are. And you painted this.

Jack   Really? A genuine Vermeer?

Mason   Of course not.

Jack   It looks wrong.

Mason   It is wrong. It's a reproduction. You painted it. It's *your* Vermeer.

Jack   I don't own a Vermeer.

Mason   It's not a Vermeer.

Jack   That's what I'm saying, you fucking idiot. How could it be? Good God. Is that a Van Gogh?

Mason   No, it's . . .

Jack   Is it?

Mason (*surrenders*)   Yes.

Jack   A Van Gogh?

Mason   Yes.

Lucy   Is it?

Mason   No.

Jack   Hello, hello. That's um . . . .

Mason   A Rembrandt.

Jack   Don't be absurd. It's one of mine. You're going bloody senile, boy.

Mason   They're all yours. You painted them all.

Jack   Now you come to mention it.

Mason   He's taking the piss half the time, is what I think.

Jack   I don't care what you think. I own a Renoir.

Mason   He did, in fact. Couldn't afford the insurance; he had to sell it.

Jack   I suppose you're the bloody imbecile who hung all these in the same gallery. What possible commonality did you intuit?

Mason   What they have in common is *you*.

Jack   They have nothing in common. They share neither content, style, nor execution. No! No, no, no; I tell a lie. Their commonality *is* their subject matter; or rather the *matter* of their subject, and what matters is *light*. How the light falls. How it bounces, how it dances, how it rests. They're all three painting light itself. Weathering the storm of their sight to bring the world to stillness. I thought if I could see it through their eyes, I might eventually see it through my own. (*Pats his pockets.*) Have you *seen* my eyes?

Mason   In your head, where you left them.

Jack   I mean glasses.

Mason   Pocket.

Jack   What a terrible thing it would be to misplace one's eyes. For God's sake, Mason, don't let me lose those.

Mason   I won't.

Jack (*genuinely fearful*)   Promise me, Mason; don't let me hand them to some idiot script supervisor to leave in a field somewhere.

Mason   I won't.

Jack   Fuck knows what I'd do without them.

Jack *has put on his glasses and turns to one of the film star portraits.*

Jack   Now her I recognise. And this one's familiar. They're all . . . I know these women.

Mason   Yes, you do. You did. You knew these women very well.

Jack   Don't tell your mother.

Mason   She already knows.

Jack   Not the half of it she doesn't.

Mason   Oh, I think she does. It's you doesn't know the half of what she knows.

He looks at the poster for The African Queen.

Jack   Bogie. Good man. 'I'm not worried, Miss. I gave myself up for dead back where we started.' Katie. This is Katie, back then.

Mason   That was then; this is now.

Jack   You know; the service in this place is appalling. I'm going to the um –

Mason   No. Dad.

Jack   Killed the dragon.

Mason   No.

Jack   The George.

Mason   Not right now.

Jack   You've got to stop fucking me about, Mason. You said we'd meet in the pub.

Mason   Yes, I did. Last Tuesday.

Jack   If you need me that's where I'll be!

Mason   You can't spend your life in the pub! You should be working, not dithering about!

Jack   I'm not dithering. I've a thirst to quench. A dragon to kill.

He strides out without ceremony.

Lucy   Shall I go after him?

Mason   No need. The way to the pub is the last thing he'll forget.

Lucy   I don't think I'm allowed to let him wander.

Mason   It's a small village. There's always someone to point him home.

Lucy   But I'm not allowed.

Mason   Good. Have you the necessary?

Lucy   Oh. Yes.

Lucy *gives* **Mason** *some scrumpled forms and an ID card.*

Lucy   You have to look at these, and then sign this to say you've seen them.

Mason   You can drive then?

Lucy   Yes, but I can't drive him.

Mason   First aid. Good.

Lucy   Yes, but I'm not registered. If he wants a paracetamol I can't give him it.

Mason   Really?

Lucy   If he wants a paracetamol I have to get him to the GP. Or phone you, so you can come home and give it to him.

Mason   Well, that's ridiculous.

Lucy   That's just . . . . that's what.

Mason   In any case; you've done the training.

Lucy   I did the three days.

Mason   Three days?

Lucy   Well, it's two and a half. But I got 82. Well, second time I . . . It's a distinction, 82 per cent.

Mason   Care in the fucking community.

Lucy   That's me. I'm good at it. I promise.

Mason   Are you at least Word literate?

Lucy   . . . the usual amount of words, I suppose.

Mason   Word-processing.

Lucy   Oh. Yes.

Mason   As we discussed.

Lucy   Yes.

Mason   It's an enhanced salary.

Lucy   I know. That's . . . Thank you.

Mason *has found a laminated chart in her documents.*

Mason   What's this?

Lucy   Oh that's . . . that's not for you. That's for me.

Mason   Faces.

Lucy   It's . . . well, it's stupid.

Mason   What is it?

Lucy   They ask you; they give it to you and they ask . . .

Mason   What?

Lucy   Well – which face do you think is a dangerous face?

Mason   A dangerous face?

Lucy   Which face?

Mason   That one.

Lucy   No. That's just an unhappy face. That's the dangerous face.

Mason   He looks quite jolly.

Lucy   I think that's the point.

Mason   My father's condition is progressive. Which is a misnomer if ever I heard one. Dementia set in a few months ago; it can only get worse, not better. And we think his eyesight may be failing. Which is another symptom of the disease.

Lucy   Does he know who he is?

Mason   Mostly, sometimes not.

Lucy   Does he know who you are?

Mason   Sometimes, mostly not.

Lucy   Most of the time does he know where he is?

Mason   Well, that depends.

Lucy   On what?

Mason   On where he is. He quite likes being in the pub, whether he is or not. Little bathroom through there. Full of dark room equipment, but usable. This door needs oiling; I'll get round to that.

Lucy   So . . . is this his room from now on?

Mason   No, no, no. Lord no. We're not fucking Eskimos. I'm not leaving him on the tundra. His room's in the house. This is meant to be his inner sanctum. In an outside garage sort of a way. His life.

Lucy   Well, he seemed to like his first look at it.

Mason   First look? I've brought him here every morning for a week.

Lucy   Oh.

Mason   As I said on the phone, we advertised for private care because beyond the obvious caring we expect you to keep him occupied.

Lucy   Yes.

Mason   To keep him focused on this.

Lucy   What is it?

Mason   He's writing a book, but it's taking too long. He'd rather *live* in the past than remember it.

Lucy   Not by choice. It's a common symptom.

Mason   I don't want it all to disappear. I want it written down. My father's lived one hell of a life.

Lucy   What sort of life?

Mason   My father made films.

Lucy   Oh.

Mason   He made some very famous films.

Lucy   Old films?

Mason   Well yes, I suppose.

Lucy   I don't like old films.

Mason   What do you mean, you don't like old films?

Lucy   I don't watch old films.

Mason   Well, I'd keep that to yourself if I were you.

Jack *returns.*

Jack   Mason?

Mason   In here.

Jack   Mason!

Mason   What is it?

Jack   The bloody pub's gone.

Mason   It's what?

Jack   It's not there.

Mason   You can't have forgotten the way to the pub.

Jack   I haven't forgotten the bloody way; I know the way.
I walked that way. The pub's not there.

Mason   It's just up the road . . .

Jack   Back to the house, turn to the – one you write with –
right!

Mason   But, you were facing the house.

Jack   Yes. And I turned *left*. Don't try to fucking confuse me.
The bloody pub's not there.

He has come in, **Mason** *has gone out.*

Mason   Dad, come here.

Jack (*beginning to panic*)   How does a bloody pub disappear?

Mason   Come here.

Jack   I've been going to that pub for forty years. What have
they done with *the fucking pub*?

Mason   Calm down. See the truck?

Jack   The truck?

Mason   The grips truck.

Jack   I know a grips truck when I see it.

Mason   It's in front of the pub.

Jack   That's Ronnie's truck by the looks of it.

Mason   The pub's behind it.

Jack   Is what?

Mason   They parked the truck in front of the George. You'd need to walk around it.

Long silence. **Jack** *comes in. Sits down.*

Jack   I'll have a scotch and soda.

Mason   In the cabinet.

Jack   You're the one that wee'd in the sink.

Lucy   No, I'm not.

Jack   Who are you, then?

Mason   This is Lucy.

Jack   Ah! 'Eh Lucy; I'm home!'

Mason   Get him a drink.

Lucy   A drink?

Mason   Scotch and soda.

Lucy   I'm not sure I'm supposed to . . .

Mason   Add it to your job description.

Lucy   You don't mind if he drinks?

Mason   It doesn't seem to make much of a difference.

Jack   What happened to the blonde one?

Mason   Who?

Jack   The one who wouldn't do it for a watch. Or the other one.

Mason   The other who?

Jack   Barmaid.

Mason   She's not a barmaid.

Jack   Then what's she doing behind the bar? Where *is* the fucking bar?

Mason   We're not in the pub. We're in the garage.

Jack   Are we?

Mason   Yes.

Jack   Well, that proves my bloody point!

Lucy   I'm Lucy. I'm going to be helping you out with this and that.

Jack   With which and what?

Lucy   With all sorts.

Jack *notices her nose-ring.*

Jack   Is that an earring in your nose?

Lucy   It's a nose ring.

Jack   She's got an earring in her nose. Does it hurt?

Lucy   It did, yes. But it doesn't.

Jack   Is this the only one?

Mason   Yes. You'll just have to put up with her.

His phone rings. It's the Pearl and Dean theme.

Sorry.

Jack   Haven't been to the cinema in an age. Couldn't get down the aisle, knee deep in popcorn.

Mason (*on the phone*)   Yes, Jonty. Hi.

Jack   Family had a picnic in the row behind. Girl had a long chat on the phone with the woman who does her nails.

Mason   Yes, I'm two minutes away. Oh, um, yes. Half a bitter. Thanks. Two minutes.

Jack   Is the pub open?

Mason   No, it isn't. You're staying here. Chapter Two; remember?

Jack   Remember?

Mason   Bad choice of words.

Jack   Remember what?

Mason   Lucy's here to help. Scotch? She's going to sit at the desk and you're going to tell her all about Technicolor. Or Garbo. Or Bogart. Tell her about *The African Queen*.

Jack   I'm no writer.

Mason   But you love talking. It's like talking, except you write it down. You talk; she writes. That's the general idea.

Jack   I'd go so far as to say; this non-existent book has *done my fucking head in*.

Mason   No. Emloid beta plaque in your hippocampus has done your head in. Remembering's good for you.

Jack   What's the bloody time then, if the pub's closed?

Mason (*to* **Lucy**)   Try not to let his mind wander.

Lucy   Well, we were told that . . .

Mason   Just do your best.

Jack   Bloody Harold Wilson. It's the winter of my discontent, I know that much.

Mason   I have to run. Good luck. (*To* **Jack**.) I'll see you later.

Jack   Righto.

Mason *leaves, closing and ducking under the door.*

Jack   Who *is* that?

Lucy   Your son.

Jack   Is it?

Lucy   Yes.

Jack   Ha. My hysterical son. Barely knows where he *is* half the time. What's this?

Lucy   Scotch and soda?

Jack   Did it get a glimpse of the scotch bottle on it's way over?

Lucy   I'm not a barmaid.

Jack   What's your speed?

Lucy   My what?

Jack   With your fingers . . . Bloody book. I was hoping to get to the end of my life before I die. Now it's bloody endless. Get on the − thing you hit with your fingers − it's got letters all over it. You press them; it makes up words.

Lucy   Oh, keyboard.

Jack   Eh?

Lucy   Where?

Jack   There.

Lucy   What's that?

Jack   Huh! You tell me.

Lucy   Oh, blimey.

Jack   That belonged to Robert Bolt and er . . . Lovely couple, but if she serves you a Chardonnay, don't drink it.

Lucy   Why not?

Jack   Never mind. Sit there.

Lucy   I'm not a typist.

Jack   What's the last sentence?

Lucy   Um . . . 'The magical component of the Technicolor camera was an ingenious . . .'

Jack   Prism. A ninety-degree prism, which wrought a miracle with light. You're not typing.

Lucy   Well, I can do two fingers but . . . I'm better with my thumbs.

Jack   Prism.

Tap. Tap. Pause.

Lucy   How do you . . .

Jack   P. R. I.

Tap.

Lucy   Ow.

Jack   . . . Thing in the sky.

Lucy   The sun?

Jack   Begins with it.

Lucy   S?

Jack   Obviously.

Tap.

Jack   Um . . . Her.

He points at the picture of Marilyn Monroe.

Lucy   That's um . . .

Jack   Marilyn.

Lucy   M.

Jack   Marilyn. Yes.

Tap.

Lucy   Prism.

Tap.

Full stop.

Jack   A ninety-degree prism . . .

Space. Tap. Space.

Lucy   Ninety the number or ninety the word?

Jack   The bloody number.

Tap. Tap. Pause.

Lucy   Degree in words or the little round thing?

Jack   The little round thing!

Lucy   Um . . .

Jack   I'm losing the will to live here.

Triumphant tap. Space. Tap. Tap. Tap. Tap. Tap!

Lucy   . . . a ninety-degree prism; what?

Jack   What?

Lucy   The prism what?

Jack   Did miracles.

Tap. Tap. Tap. Space. Tap.

Enough.

Tap.

Desist! Can you take dictation?

Lucy   I can write faster than I can type.

Jack   Where on God's earth did the studio find you?

Lucy   My office skills are limited. I'm sorry. Please don't tell him. I really need this job.

Jack   Hoping to be discovered by Michael Powell on your way to the canteen? Looking for a casting couch to fall across? If you are, this is the one, by the way. This is the actual casting couch everyone talks about.

Lucy   That's inappropriate, Jack.

Jack   I'm teasing, nurse.

Lucy   I'm not a nurse.

Jack   Well that's bloody obvious.

Lucy   I lied about the office skills but I'm a good carer.

Jack   You think?

Lucy   I fucking care, alright?

Jack   I don't need taking fucking care of. I need this bloody
. . . thing you read words in . . .

Lucy   Book.

Jack   . . . book off my . . . thing you eat your dinner off . . .

Lucy   Plate.

Jack   Plate. I'm supposed to be meeting John Huston for
lunch.

Lucy   There's a thing here. A whatsit, a dictaphone.

Jack   No no no – use your fingers like anyone else. Ha ha!
That's definitely the punch line; you must have buggered up
the feed. There used to be holes, in the dial, you see, for your
fingers; not your dick, of course. That was the gag.

Lucy   So shall we use your dictaphone?

Jack   Ha ha! You see? The old ones are the best. In light of
your staggering ineptitude on the – finger-pressing thing, I
suppose we must.

Lucy   Why don't you just say whatever comes into your
head. I'll type it up later.

Click.

Jack   What was I talking about?

Lucy   The prism.

Jack   The prism splits the light. Imagine a – jolly thing when
it's raining –

Lucy   Umbrella?

Jack   Up in the sky.

Lucy   Rainbow?

Jack   A rainbow of just three colours. When we first shot in colour the film was slow; you had to blast the hell out of everything. Technicolor solved it. This was how. This is her. The old Rolls-Royce. This beauty puts light through its paces. You run three strips of − damn! − you can see through it −

Lucy   Glass?

Jack   Goes in a camera!

Lucy   Film!

Jack   FILM! You run three strips of *film* through this creature simultaneously, so you only need one-third of the light. Light goes through the lens and hits the − the, er −

Lucy   The prism.

Jack   The prism. And the prism does its magic. One beam goes straight ahead, passes through a − grass − Irish − *green* filter, which blocks the red and blue, and forms an image on your first strip of panchromatic . . . *panchromatic*, how about them apples! Panchromatic film. The other beam turns ninety degrees left and passes through a magenta filter, which blocks the green light, and forms an image on a − two strips of film running through the camera together − you won't know this − no one knew this − they invented it − a *bi-pack!* The red/blue bipack. The front film sensitive only to the blue end of the Dulux. − Rainbow. − Spectrum! You following this?

Lucy   I got lost when something turned left.

Jack   Were you blonde yesterday?

Lucy   No.

Jack   It suited you.

Lucy   I wasn't and it wouldn't. What turned left?

Jack   Sixty-six per cent of the light turned left. So you've got your green and you've got your blue, but here's the thing . . . the blue strip has a red filter which means the second strip of film behind it only records the red end. So you end up with three negatives; cyan, magenta and . . . custard.

Lucy   Custard?

Jack   Mustard.

Lucy   Yellow.

Jack   Yellow, ha ha, and you superimpose all three on to a single strip of film and *voilà*, you have a full-colour projection print.

Lucy   It sounds very impressive.

Jack   Look at her. She's oiled and buffed, still perfectly calibrated. She's ready to turn over, but she's . . . me.

Lucy   She's yours?

Jack   No, she's me, she's . . . finished. She's defunct. Nothing left to run through her, and she's lost her crystal – beats in the chest.

Lucy   Her heart?

Jack   Her crystal heart. It's broken. Before they let us touch a prism, they made us practise with wooden blocks. They made us practise dropping the buggers. Given a fair wind I could still catch one on my foot. First time I held one and turned it in the light; it did what the Impressionists struggled a lifetime to do: it embraced the light, split the light; it seemed to understand *the very secret of light* . . . I thought, this isn't an optical instrument I'm holding here. This is – oh, Lord – big chap, white beard, sits in heaven.

Lucy   God.

Jack   God. God's geometric eyeball. I was holding God's eyeball in the palm of my hand.

Lucy   Can I see it?

Jack   Haven't got it.

Lucy   Where is it?

Jack   Mason fucking dropped it.

Lucy   Oops.

Jack   You are the mistress of understatement. I've forgiven him. It was years ago. Haven't been offered a decent film since. Don't try to tell me that's a coincidence. But she and I, in our day, we captured some light. One end of the spectrum to the other and a few colours along the way we invented for ourselves. That green jacket in the gallery of *The Red Shoes*; those shades of purple I wove through *Black Narcissus*. No one had seen those colours before, because no one had *photographed* those damn colours before. Before she and I came along.

Lucy   They're old films, right?

Jack   Who are you again?

Lucy   I'm Lucy.

Jack   Lucy! What's your favourite film?

Lucy   I haven't got one.

Jack   You must have. What's your favourite old film?

Lucy   I don't like old films.

Jack   You don't what?

Lucy   I don't watch them.

Jack   You don't watch old films?

Lucy   They're too long.

Jack   Too long?!

Lucy   Some of them are really long. And they don't fit the telly.

Jack   Are you pulling my dick?

Lucy   Language.

Jack   You must have watched a few.

Lucy   To the end?

Jack   Surely to God?

Lucy   Not really. You sit through a comedy and it's not funny and it's happy ever after, which it never is. Or you watch something serious; some bloke goes through all sorts of shit then gets home and plays baseball with his kid. Horror: the blonde gets cut up, the brunette gets away. The end. Happy or dead. Films are bollocks.

Jack   In the face of such an articulate summation I shall happily concede that films are bollocks. But I'll go further; novels come out of a horse's . . . whatever it is. Paintings are pitiful daubs, poetry is tedious doggerel. World culture is a pile of steaming, odious crap. In fact if I were to meet the – man in a cave – caveman – Neanderthal! who first uttered a fairy tale, I'd brain him with a femur. Perhaps you'd like to poke my eyes out with a stick?

Lucy   You've been lucky. Nice house. Pictures. You've forgotten. Life's not like in films. Life just goes on and on. And it's only got one ending.

They stare at each other.

Jack   Life is temporary. Film is forever.

Lucy   If you say so.

Jack   You know, John Huston once said to me: 'We've all got a strip of celluloid running through us. It's got a thousand images on it and it's a fragile thing. But if you're an artist you are going to cut and colour and grade and project that celluloid back at the world, because our past is all we've got to give.' Our stories are the heart of us.

Lucy   Not mine.

Jack   What's your story?

Lucy   I haven't got one.

Jack   You must have. Once upon a time; what's the first thing you remember?

Lucy   Once upon a time, my mother drowned. A stupid trip to Camber Sands. A stupid rubber swim-cap. A riptide. I was eight.

Jack   Chapter two.

Lucy   Night of her funeral my dad sat on my bed and told me a story about her. The next night I made him invent another chapter. Night after night that went on, until he was making most of it up. I thought her story would never end. A year later he overdosed himself with paracetemol and whisky, and there were no more stories.

Jack   I'm sorry.

Lucy   So I don't like stories.

Jack   And yet telling them is what you chose. You chose to share yourself. You're conflicted, understandably, which is probably why you can never turn up on time.

Lucy   I'm always on time.

Jack   Tell that to the crew.

Lucy   I'm sorry?

Jack   I'm joking. We all love you.

Lucy   Love who?

Jack   It's the rest of the profession think you're a pain in the backside.

Lucy   I see.

Jack   Don't let your spools work loose. You'll end up all over the cutting-room floor.

Nicola *enters through the small door. A bird-like woman. The bearing of a thrush and the courage of a robin.*

Nicola   Hello, Jack.

Jack   I'm not here!

Nicola   Yes you are.

Jack (*instantly brightening*)   Katie!

Nicola   You must be Lucy.

Jack   Climb aboard! Katie; this is . . .

Lucy   Lucy.

Jack   Lucy.

Nicola   I'm Nicola. Hello.

Lucy   Hello.

Jack   Lucy, this is Katie.

Nicola   Not Katie, Jack.

Jack   Are you feeling better? Katie drank the water. She's not been feeling herself.

Nicola   I'm feeling fine.

Jack   Bogart's playing poker with Huston. Ugly and Double-Ugly. We'll lose the sun in half an hour.

Nicola   You're not shooting, Jack.

Jack   I've had no one to shoot!

Nicola   Though I'm not surprised you're confused, Mason having installed you in your own museum.

Jack   While we're waiting, maybe another martini.

Nicola   How do you like it?

Jack   Dirty!

Nicola   Not the drink. All this.

Jack   It's a bloody jungle. I might not get out alive. Clapper loader fell overboard.

Nicola   That was forty years ago.

Jack   Where's my damn Tewe?

Nicola   Where did you leave it?

Jack   In my lens box. Where's my lens box?

Nicola   Is that it, over there? One of those?

Jack   What's it doing in the bloody prow?

Jack *sorts through his lens boxes, checking lenses, polishing them.*

Nicola   Nicola's my name. Most of the time he hasn't a clue who I am. Although he occasionally remembers who I was.

Lucy   As a child?

Nicola   Well, that's very flattering of you, dear; but I'm not his daughter, I'm his wife.

Lucy   Oh, Christ. Sorry.

Nicola   You're entitled to be surprised, but not appalled.

Lucy   I'm neither, honestly.

Nicola   I'm sorry I wasn't here to say hello. They're controlling traffic in the village for *Midsomer* bloody *Murders*. How are you coping so far?

Lucy   We're getting on, I think.

Nicola   All this is Mason's idea. I don't think it's good for Jack, all this wallowing in the past.

Lucy   Well, there's a school of thought that . . .

Nicola   Jack needs looking after. In a dispassionate manner, as opposed to the familial manner, which for all our efforts, doesn't seem to do him a whole lot of good. Mason has worn us all out trying to keep Jack in the present so that he can write about the past. Which is an irony totally lost on Mason, let alone Jack.

Jack   I think I should warn you: no one ever did find that other black mamba. Ernie's got peritonitis. Local runner finally turned up; bloke's a bloody leper. Sent him packing.

Nicola   You're not in the jungle, Jack. You're in the garage. Just look around you!

Jack   Well this won't do. That's a tin roof. You can't shoot raincover under a tin roof.

Nicola   You're not shooting.

Jack   Of course we're not! Bloody monsoon.

Lucy   Maybe if you . . .

Nicola   I admit I'm exhausted.

Jack   Thank Christ these boxes are watertight. Could have lost the lot.

Nicola   You're not on the river.

Jack   Bogie's a boatman. They should listen to him. You can't make a raft with a 200-amp gennie on it turn sharp right. I almost yelled 'Cut!'

Nicola   Jack . . .

Jack   Bloody stupid not to. Bloody proud I didn't. (*Gets increasingly anxious.*) We should be turning over. We've got sod-all in the can! Betty's got Bogie by the balls. Huston wants to shoot a lion; I hope it's fucking eaten him.

Nicola   Please, Jack . . .

Jack   Sodding mosquitos! Where's my bloody camera crew?

Lucy   They've gone for tea.

Jack   For what?

Lucy   For tea.

Jack   Tea?

Lucy   It's the tea break.

Jack   Is it? Good. I'll have a martini.

Calm again, he polishes lenses.

Nicola   I'd rather you didn't indulge him.

Lucy   It calmed him.

Nicola   I prefer Jack in the present.

Lucy   That's not always best.

Nicola   I hate to see him so confused.

Lucy   I've got a pamphlet. He sounds confused to you because you're here and he's in the jungle or whatever. If you insist he's in the garage, you really confuse him.

Nicola   So, Jack thinks he's in the pub, and I should what? Put on my barmaid's smile and serve him a scotch?

Lucy   It's what I was told.

Nicola   My husband is hanging over the edge of a cliff. It's not an easy thing to let go.

Lucy   Maybe you could jump with him.

Jack   Huston and Bogie tied one on last night.

Lucy   Did they?

Jack   Indeed they did.

Lucy   Well, that's men for you.

Nicola (*to* **Lucy**)   If I'm to be honest; we fell over that cliff some time ago.

Jack   We're going to lose the light.

Nicola   I have little hope we'll climb back up.

Lucy   If that's where he wants to be . . .

Jack   I'm not waiting for the bastards any longer. Katie; I'm going to shoot your close-up.

Nicola   Well, Jack, I wouldn't want to disappoint you.

Jack   She'll need a bit of a touch-up. Take that shine off her forehead.

Nicola   Make-up, then. For the make-believe.

Lucy   Right.

She rummages in her bag.

Jack   This one doesn't like make-believe. This one thinks our entire profession is a sham. If we weren't nine hundred miles from civilisation I'd make her walk back. And lips; she needs some lips.

Nicola   The lightest purple.

Jack   As ever was.

He gets to work setting up the Technicolor camera.

Here she is. I am so proud of you. Humidity, pollen. You're coping with the Congo better than any of us. So Huston calls me, we do scotch and cigars, he says, 'We put the boat on a raft, and we float down the Congo.' I say, 'What about the generator?' He says, 'Who needs lamps? Africa's where the sun is.' Ignoramus. So we build a second raft. So that's Africa, water, electricity, and you. A recipe for complete disaster. Look at that river. Ten million years of decaying trees and vegetation. Those malignant-looking vines, like tentacles. And beware those rotting trees; like sleeping crocodiles, because the sleeping crocodiles look just like rotting trees. You know, if I use a fifty I'll be in the damn river.

Nicola   If you use a thirty-five, I'll push you in the damn river.

Jack   Darling Katie. Why don't you and I jump ship?

Nicola   Because the water's black as squid ink, and I'm not who you think I am.

Jack   But that's your charm. None of us quite know who you are.

Nicola   And who am I, Jack?

Jack (*pause*)   You know, if you look hard at the water it's not black; it's the deepest green. You're not really going to get in it, are you?

Nicola   Never in a thousand years. Or possibly first thing in the morning. Whatever's on the schedule; you know me.

Jack   That water's lethal. You might never be seen again.

Nicola   Set up the shot, Jack.

Lucy *has found her make-up and touches* **Nicola** *up.* **Jack** *arranges a key light and a highlight.*

Jack   And how are we feeling today? Wistfully emotive?

Nicola   If you'd be so kind.

Jack   Chin high?

Nicola   High chin, indeed.

Jack   Gaffer's in hospital, in Nairobi. Focus puller's in the dunny. Been there for hours.

Nicola   Maybe the leper could lend a hand.

Jack   No thanks. I'll do it myself. Tell you the truth; I'd rather.

Nicola   Then let's just do the set-up, dear.

Jack *measures focus.*

Nicola   Let's not be too precise. A gentleman photographer is always a little fuzzy round the edges.

Jack *looks through the camera.*

Jack   Tilt up. A little more.

Nicola   My eyes are dry.

Jack   I know what you need.

Nicola   What's that?

Jack   You need a little of this.

Nicola   You keep a menthol stick in your old lens bag?

Jack   I keep *your* menthol stick in my old lens bag.

Pause.

Nicola   You kept her old menthol stick?

Jack   Call me sentimental.

Nicola   Seriously; you did?

Jack   I did.

Nicola   That seems rather . . . perverse.

Jack   A souvenir.

Nicola   A rather perverse souvenir.

Jack   Do you think so?

Nicola   . . . I'd rather you'd stolen an old silk slip, or something less . . .

Jack   Less?

Nicola   Intimate.

She takes the menthol stick. **Jack** *makes final adjustments to the key light.*

Jack   Did I tell you Marlene's trick?

Nicola   White line down the middle of her turned-up pixie nose?

Jack   Nope. Just before turn over?

Nicola   What?

Jack   Gold dust.

Nicola   No!

Jack   Pure twenty carat. Just a little sprinkling.

Nicola   The bitch.

Jack   Don't fret. You are peerless.

Nicola   I am freckled. I'm no beauty, I know.

Jack   You shine from within.

Nicola   I do no such thing. I rely on you to shine upon me.

Jack   Katie's key light is a little lower than most. And we shall need a little accent at lens height.

Nicola   To catch the crocodile tears.

Jack   You mean they're not entirely genuine?

Nicola   Mum's the word.

She uses the menthol stick, blinks, eyes glistening.

Jack   I could rarely make you laugh, Katie. But I could always help you cry.

Nicola   *Almost* cry. Actual tears would be rather cheap, don't you think?

Jack (*to* **Lucy**)   New girl; look through here. (*To* **Nicola**.) Just . . . the chin . . . May I?

Lucy *looks through the camera.* **Jack** *lifts* **Nicola***'s chin an iota.*

Lucy   Oh my God.

Nicola   What?

Lucy   You look amazing.

Jack   She does, doesn't she. Katie?

Nicola   Oh, Jack . . .

Lucy   Don't spoil it.

Jack   Why don't you and I . . . have an affair?

Nicola   Because you're married, Jack.

Jack   But Katie, you're the one.

Nicola   That's a lie. I hope you know.

Mason *returns through small door.* **Nicola** *wipes her eyes.*

Mason   Dad?

Jack   What the hell are you doing here?

Mason   Good God. What are you up to?

Jack   You're not resilient enough for the jungle, boy; you'll catch everything going.

Mason   We're in Africa again, are we?

Jack   Dysentery's not the half of it.

Mason   I think I'm safe; I'm not born yet.

Jack   The clapper loader's got fucking malaria.

Mason   You're in Denham, Dad! And there's a chap in the pub wants to meet you.

Jack   The pub?

Nicola   Mason . . .

Mason   I thought you might like to go to the pub.

Jack (*instantly brightening*)   Righto. I'll just shake a few dew drops off the lily.

He disappears into the bathroom.

Mason   He shouldn't be fooling with this.

Nicola   He was perfectly content.

Mason   He was in the bloody jungle.

Nicola   Lucy feels we should let him be wherever he thinks he is.

Mason   Well, that's bloody ridiculous.

Lucy   It's what I was taught. It's what you need to . . .

Mason   He needs hanging on to, not letting go.

Nicola   Who is it wants to meet him?

Mason   Jonty Robbins wants to meet him.

Nicola   And this results in what?

Mason   A drink or two. A chance to live the glory days.

Nicola   Jack seven sails to the wind again in his inglenook of adoring sycophants.

Mason   He enjoys it.

Nicola   Being used. A conduit for other's careers.

Mason   It's not like that.

Nicola   Oh, I know Jack. Jack and I go way back. I'm a friend of Jack's.

Mason   That's unfair.

Jack *emerges.*

Jack   Shall we meet her there? Because you realise we could wait all day? The level of a woman's self-confidence is in inverse proportion to the time she keeps you waiting. For this one (*Sophia*) it was just the odd five minutes of blissful anticipation. This one (*Marlene*) was a wily bird. She'd arrive bang on time, then keep you waiting longer than all the rest. She'd make a punctual entrance and then slow down time itself. But this one (*Marilyn*) well, we wasted entire days of our lives waiting for this one. She hoarded time, but when she finally arrived to spend it was always bewildered that in the eyes of cast and crew her wealth had considerably *de*creased.

Nicola   And what about in your eyes, Jack?

Jack   I'm less of a fool.

Nicola   You had the patience of the devil.

Jack   You might be the only one that got away.

Nicola   Is that entirely true?

Jack   Our hearts are not enough; you want the time of our lives. In little increments. So you'll take half an hour of it just choosing a – you take it off – *dress*. Dress, for dinner. My first wife was the worst. That didn't last long. Long enough for Mason to come along; that was about it. Short and sour.

Nicola   Jack managed to be a little reconstructed during the late eighties, but it wore off again.

Mason   She did say she'd meet us there.

Jack   Where?

Mason   Down the pub.

Jack   Righto.

Nicola   Oh, Mason.

Jack   Who? Not Marlene; she wouldn't do a pub.

Mason   It's a surprise.

Jack   Excellent. I'm good at those. Sophia! She doesn't mind slumming it.

Nicola   Don't let him order doubles.

Jack   I'm an idiot. (*To* **Lucy**.) It's you. Of course it's you. You know the pub. You taught them what a cosmo was. Make-up are ready for you. We'll need half an hour to set up. You know one day, you and I should do some stills.

Jack *and* **Mason** *begin to leave.*

Jack   This would make a hell of a crane shot, pull back and up, swing round with us; you'd get the church and the pub, entire village. (*Off.*) If you could cope with heights, of course . . .

Mason (*off*)   I can cope with heights.

Jack (*off*)   You bloody well can't. We'll rig you a safety net.

Lucy   Should I go with them?

Nicola   Getting rat-arsed in the pub is not part of your job description, any more than being Katharine Hepburn is part of mine. Mason hired you to get the book done, didn't he?

Lucy   Well no; I'm a Care Assistant. I'm qualified. But yes –
some secretarial was part of what we – what Mr Cardiff – but
I am a qualified carer.

Nicola   Consider that your priority, please. Mason inherited
from Jack the quaint presumption that all women enjoy doing
whatever needs doing. Whatever their chosen occupation.

Lucy   Are you an actress?

Nicola   Good heavens no. I was a PA. Jack needed a PA. I
mean, he *needed* a PA. Always did. Still does, always will. I think
only one of us was ever daft enough to actually sleep with him.
And I'd rather you didn't.

Lucy   I wasn't going to.

Nicola   Good. I don't know if he's been faithful but I don't
much care, because I've been his and he's been mine.

Lucy   Have you been married long?

Nicola   Half my life. I'm not at all sure it should have
happened, Jack and I. He was a rather senior figure in his own
life, let alone mine. I was a wild child. Which denotes a sense
of freedom, but I was far from free. No self-confidence; my
liberal behaviour was a defence. Then I met Jack. He was
married to Mason's mother. The marriage was everything a
marriage should be, and miserable to boot. We'd take long
walks, and he'd confide. He'd slept with film stars, it
transpired.

Lucy   Oh.

Nicola   It was just a hobby. He was English, you see. And
he was the man who made them beautiful. It was a hard hand
to beat if he played the cards right, and he played them to
perfection. So be warned. He showed me all his card tricks,
and then dealt a hand in my direction. I was twenty-seven
years old and there were twenty-seven years between us. Come
to Daddy, he said. And I did. A newspaper called me his hippy

strumpet. We adopted the title. We adored each other. It was a shock that the memories of me were the first to go.

Lucy   I'm sorry. It's none of my business.

Nicola   Well, that's the joy of strangers, is it not? We're none of each other's business.

Jack *returns, followed by* **Mason**.

Jack   Ceiling's too ruddy low in there and it's fixed to the walls. They fixed it to the bloody walls. I can't get a key light in there above eight feet and when she does arrive, if she ever arrives, she's going to hit that fucking ceiling, which doesn't fly. I can't do it. The floor's uneven; they haven't put a floor down, a track won't do, I need to dolly. Mason's not the best, but with a floor down he'd have coped. And they've piled in the extras before I've even reccied the damn place. You know who's sitting there? She hates strangers on set and you know who's sitting there? The President of the United States. How . . . insensitive can you bloody well get?

Mason   Dad, his name's Jonty and the chap's in awe of you; you should at least have the decency to speak to him . . .

Jack   You know he's trying to screw your wife.

Mason   He's what?

Jack   And she's bloody terrified of him!

Nicola (*to* **Mason**)   See what you've done; he was perfectly calm.

Jack   These men have power; you've no idea. She's going to wake up in the Canoga River! She's going to wake up with needle holes between her toes. *I predict it!*

Nicola   Would you like another cocktail?

Jack   He's put her in mortal danger!

Nicola   Damn you, Mason; why can't you leave him in peace?

Mason   He likes to meet people.

Nicola   Not any more. Not industry people. It fills him with anxiety, and this is where we end up.

Jack (*beginning to panic*)   Stay away from the pub. Don't trust any of them. It's one thing to my face, another behind my back. Bloody rubbish they made me shoot over the years. All a conspiracy – because I know things; do you see? I could tell a tale or two. I know you couldn't care less; you don't like make-believe. Well, I've news for you; your entire life is make-believe! The truth lies beneath and it's going to kill you. That man is going to have you killed. Don't ask me how I know, but they know I know which is why we're both in danger. Close that bloody door, for Christ's sake; they're all in the pub!

Nicola   Jack; calm down.

Jack   It's the story they don't want told. I should be shooting it but this thing's bloody useless, and even if we find the stock for her, she's got no sodding prism.

Mason   Dad, you're not shooting. You've nothing to shoot.

Jack   You dropped the fucking thing! It was thirty years old; it was pretty nigh unique, and you dropped it!

Nicola   Jack . . .

Jack   You couldn't even get your foot to it. You imbecile. I can't do a bloody thing without it. You wrecked my fucking career! You want to build your own out of the wreckage, well you can't. There's no sodding prism!

Nicola   Jack . . . .

Jack   I can barely see without it!

Nicola   Jack! Sing us a song.

Jack   What?

Nicola   One of your father's old songs.

Jack   One of Dad's ol' songs?

Nicola Why not, Jack?

Jack (*to* **Mason**) He never thought I could, you see. He didn't want me living in his shadow. (*To* **Lucy**.) I used to stand in the wings, you see.

Lucy Sing, Jack.

Jack

> The girl I love is up in the gallery . . .
> The girl I love is looking down at me . . .
>
> She's my lady love, she is my love
> My turtle dove . . .

Lucy That's nice.

Jack 'Music Hall's Last Gasp' is what he called himself.

> She's my lady love, she is my love
> My turtle dove . . .

Nicola That's lovely, Jack.

Jack
> I've got a lovely bunch of coconuts . . .

Nicola Not that one.
Jack
> There they are all standing in a row . . .
>
> There stands me wife . . .
> The idol of me life . . .
> Singing . . .

Well, this isn't going to get a film in the can, is it?

Blackout.

Scene Two

The same. **Jack** *is alone. He sits talking into the dictaphone.*

Jack   Marilyn's face was rosy, flushed with sleep. Her buttercup-gold hair tangled like a Botticelli cherub. Her eyes are the unreal clarity of the porcelain eyes in a doll, and the mouth, timorously half-parted lips, the saucy upturned nose; here indeed was a delightful evocation of Renoir. Arthur Miller, on the other hand, reminded me of Reginald Christie.

His eyes settle on the portrait of Marilyn, which smiles at him. **Lucy** *enters through the small door.*

Lucy   I'm late. I know. I'm sorry.

Jack   Never you mind.

Lucy   My mother said I was to apologise if I was even five minutes late. I spend most of my life apologising. It's not that I'm deliberately late, it's just that I get to a place and discover I am.

Jack   I was happy to wait.

Lucy   Some are, some aren't.

Jack   May I say, you are looking utterly enchanting.

Lucy   You're a gentleman, I know. But a liar.

Jack   It's true.

Lucy   I look atrocious.

Jack   Luminous.

Lucy   Sure. And I put so much effort into it. How are you today, Jack?

Jack   We had a little something planned.

Lucy   Did we?

Jack   You know we did.

He moves to his 'Vermeer'.

I was standing in front of this, the original, the day I became *conscious* of light.

He moves from the 'Vermeer' to the 'Van Gogh'.

And when I stumbled in front of this for the first time the light poured *through* my eyes and came to life inside my head.

He moves to his own stuff.

Jack   I still shuffled about like the Vaudevillian's child that I am, but my eyes were open to an elevated realm; Shiva's swirling realm of photon. Under that green canopy, on the excavated walls of Troy, at the ballet, in the desert, on the village green; even amidst the garish surround of my petty, pretty artifice . . . light has been my life. And you are made of it, and I shall capture it. Chiaroscuro is too harsh for you. A soft enveloping light is what we need. A low key light and a very gentle fill.

Lucy   I'm sure I don't know what you are talking about.

Jack   You promised.

Lucy   Yes, but if I did it was only to please you.

Jack   Then please me.

Lucy   Well, as long as you expect nothing of me. I have nothing to give. I shall just sit here like a lemon without a thought in my head.

Jack   So be it. I found a hat for you to wear.

Lucy   I don't wear hats. I look like an ice-cream sundae.

Jack   You'll like this hat.

Lucy   I won't.

Jack   You will. This is the hat.

Lucy   I love it.

He sets up lights, and his vintage Hasselblad.

Jack   I've had this beauty for twenty years.

Lucy   I hate my nose.

Jack   I know you do.

Lucy   How did you know?

Jack   You touch it a lot.

Lucy   I do not.

Jack   Well, yes you do.

Lucy   I do? Do I?

Jack   Yes.

Lucy   You think I'm hiding something?

Jack   You've nothing to hide. You are exquisite.

Lucy   Yeah. That's how I get through the day.

Jack   Incandescent.

Lucy   Like a moth.

Jack   Lie back a little.

Lucy   My favourite position. I didn't mean that the way it came out.

Jack   The thing about a hat –

Lucy   I don't wear hats.

Jack   – is it's not enough to put it on. You have to *wear* the hat.

Lucy   Could you hide my nose with the hat?

Jack   The key light that suits you most is lower than usual.

Lucy   I'll bet you say that to all the girls.

Jack   It accentuates your nose.

Lucy   Oh God, I *hate* my nose.

Jack   Thus the angle of the inky-dink.

Lucy   The inky-dink?

Jack   The lamp.

Lucy   I see.

Jack *takes a photograph.*

Lucy   I wasn't ready.

Jack   That's why I took it.

Lucy   Oh.

He takes another.

Jack   So. Were you looking at the camera or was the camera looking at you?

Lucy   Which is best?

Jack   Both are good. But you have to choose. You try to do both at once, and that's not possible.

Lucy   You're right. That's what I do.

Jack   You must leave the moment to me. Don't try to shape the moment. I will shape the moment. All you have to be . . . is in it.

They are very close. **Mason** *has entered, and is watching.*

Mason   I wouldn't entirely trust him, if I were you.

Lucy   Jack wants to immortalise me.

Mason   I'm sure that's not all he wants.

Jack   Don't jump to conclusions, my dear fellow. Art is an intimate thing.

Mason   I'm very well aware of that.

Jack   We shall both attempt to immortalise her, but between you and I, she needs no help from either of us.

Mason   Obfuscate all you like. You have this woman stretched out on a chaise . . .

Lucy   He was taking my photograph, that's all he was doing.

Jack   I wouldn't trust her either, Arthur, but I'm a gentleman. I'd keep your powder dry if I were you.

Nicola *appears. She has a mailing box with her.*

Nicola   I saw you from the window, sneaking in.

Jack   Katie! What are you doing here?

Nicola   You think you're going to take him to the pub.

Jack   Is he? Jolly good. Bury the hatchet.

Nicola   Well, you're not taking him to the pub.

Jack   Is he not? Are you at Pinewood?

Nicola   I'm your wife, Jack; and I've got something for you. It was just delivered.

Mason   I didn't come here to take him to the pub.

Jack   He came to punch me on the nose.

Mason   I just dropped by to see how the book was going.

Jack   He thinks I was attempting to seduce his wife.

Nicola   And what about Jack? How's Jack?

Jack   Spiffing, thanks.

Mason   Of course, how's Jack?

Jack   On top of the – round thing with green bits and blue bits.

Lucy   The world.

Jack   The world. And I *was* attempting to seduce his wife.

Lucy   I'm not his wife.

Jack   Don't talk bloody nonsense.

Nicola   Not as easy as it looks, is it?

Jack   And you're not even on this one! You're on the wrong bloody sound stage!

Mason   For Christ's sake, just settle down!

Jack (*suddenly aggressive*)   Would you like to punch me on the nose?

Mason   No, thank you.

Nicola   Jack!

Jack   Would fisticuffs with the Englishman assuage your displeasure?

Mason   Would they assuage your guilt?

Jack   I *adore* your wife! You don't deserve her, you pretentious scribbler! She's beyond exquisite!

Jack *grabs* **Lucy** *and gives her a Technicolor kiss.*

Nicola   Jack, no!

Mason   Steady on, now!

Jack   Take your best shot. Put one right there.

Nicola   Jack!

Jack   I sparred with Huston. Gave Hitchcock a piece of my mind. Told Rambo to go fuck himself.

Mason   You're a man to be reckoned with.

Jack   Correct!

Jack *punches* **Mason** *on the chin.*

Lucy   Oh.

Nicola   No, Jack! No.

Jack   Ow!

Nicola   Stop it now . . .

Jack   I'm Jack Cardiff!

Nicola   Yes. Yes you are. And look. This is for you.

Jack   Who?

Nicola   Look, Jack. Look and see.

Nicola *opens the mailing box.* **Jack** *looks in the box and takes out a prism. It has a profound effect on him.*

Nicola   It's a prism.

Jack   Not possible.

Nicola   Why not?

Jack   It got broken.

Nicola   It's another.

Jack   It's a prism.

Nicola   Yes.

Jack *holds it up to the light. The prism refracts a modest rainbow.*

Jack   Hold on a minute. Déjà vu.

Nicola   Leave us.

Lucy   He was taking my picture, he got confused.

Nicola   Go to the house, please.

Lucy   Yes.

Nicola   And let some daylight in.

Mason   That really hurt.

Nicola   Mason. Leave us.

Lucy *opens the main door as she and* **Mason** *leave through the small one.* **Jack** *is looking through the prism.*

Jack   Look. A prism.

Nicola   Yes.

Jack   And not a moment too soon. We're way behind schedule. (*To the Technicolor camera.*) See this, my old beauty? We'll soon have you up and running; sight restored. Mind you, it's dark in here. It's darker, is it? It got dark outside.

Nicola   We're just waiting for the sun, dear.

Jack   I won't shoot cloud all day. We'll wait for sun.

Nicola   Good call.

Jack   Scuddy days; I fucking hate them.

Thunder.

Oh Lord; rain stops play. That's the problem trying to shoot in England. You waste so much bloody time.

Nicola   Oh, you found ways to fill the time. You were happy in cloud cover so long as there was an actress and some gin.

Jack   Do you remember Africa! Lit by God. Did we ever see the sun?

Nicola   Never.

Jack   It was either pissing down or we were in some fetid jungle canyon that hadn't seen the light of day since before the dawn of time.

Nicola   We towed the sun behind us.

Jack   I lit that film too well. It should have been jungle light. Rousseau. It's . . . so dark in here.

Nicola   It's going to rain. Is all.

Loud thunder.

Jack   Can't shoot a damn thing in this light. I can't live without light. To go blind on this earth would be the torture I deserve, for having such a glorious hell of a time of it.

Nicola   You're not going blind. There's a storm due.

Jack (*beginning to panic*)   If I should go blind, smother me with a pillow. Promise me. If I can't see I don't want to live. It's the darkness I fear, not the death.

Nicola *embraces him.*

Nicola   Shh. We're just waiting for sun.

Jack   Katie. Katie?

Nicola   Mmm?

Jack   Do you think we ever know that we are dead?

Nicola   No, Jack, I do not.

The garage partially transforms. Rain and the impression of black murky water. It is dusk. Animals cry. We are on the deck of The African Queen.

End of Act One.

Act Two

Scene One

Between an unwieldy, rusty steel boiler and the helm of the boat is a small deck. Over it is stretched a tarpaulin. A light monsoon rain patters on to the tarpaulin. All around is African jungle. Below is dark, turgid water. Huddled around a crate playing poker are **Jack**, **Bogart** *and* **Bacall**. **Hepburn** *has her head over the side of the boat. The shriek of a monkey.*

Bogart   What in God's name was that?

Betty   Colobus.

Bogart   A what?

Betty   Monkey.

Bogart   Big one or little one?

Betty   Little one. The big ones are chimpanzees.

Another shriek.

There's a troupe of them surrounding us.

Bogart   Where?

Betty   Just look around you.

Bogart   What do they eat?

Betty   Colobus? Fruit. Chimpanzees; whatever they come across.

Bogart   Jesus H. Christ.

Betty   I need another drink.

Jack   Mine's a martini.

Betty   I knew we'd make a man of you.

Jack   Katie, are you feeling any better?

Katharine   Noooh.

Betty   She looks like death.

Katharine   Death would be a blessing.

Betty *puts a bucket in front of her.*

Betty   Maintain your dignity. Use a bucket.

Bogart   Drink some scotch.

Katharine   I curse you all from the depth of my being.

Bogart   I'm praying the depth of your being never misses the bucket.

Katharine   My derrière is sodden.

Bogart   I'll raise you ten.

Betty   Do you want a twist in this?

Jack   I want it dirty.

Betty   Oh, it'll be that.

Bogart   You know what those dirty ones do to you?

Jack   I'll risk it.

Betty   Katie, you sure?

Katharine   Spence once said to me I play a better drunk than any drunk he knew. It's because I always stayed sober enough to watch.

Bogart   Have it your own way. Drink the water. Throw up in the harmonium.

Katharine   Where's the damn crew?

Jack   Snug as bugs in the schoolhouse.

Katharine   And where the hell is Huston?

Bogart   Double Ugly? I'd say he was sleeping it off, but I don't think he sleeps.

Jack   He'll be in the jungle, painting something or shooting something.

Katharine   Well, if he doesn't shoot something of me soon, I'll shoot him.

Jack   I meant, with a rifle.

Katharine   So did I.

Jack   We've only ourselves to blame. He told us what we were in for.

Katharine   You maybe. He lied through his teeth to me. He promised me air conditioning and a dozen native bearers. I thought I had the title role. *The African Queen*. He didn't tell me it was the name of the boat.

Jack   He was in his cups last night.

Katharine   First time I met him he said to me, to make a film you have to *partake of life*.

Bogart   Stalk it, skin it, and hang it on the wall.

Katharine   I prefer to partake of it in Beverly Hills.

Jack   He's right though. Thanks to making movies I know all there is to know about Viking history, bull-fighting, the ballet, plastic surgery. Geisha girls. I have drunk Burgundy in Renoir's house and coffee in Cézanne's studio. In the asylum at St-Remy I gazed at the landscape beyond the barred window of Van Gogh's cell. I have stood alone in Anne Frank's room. And I have stood there with her father. He said to me he knew the name of her betrayer. I didn't ask the name. It didn't seem any of my business. Hell with the rain. We're privileged.

Katharine   Yes, we are.

Betty   I hear the malaria ward in Nairobi is a lovely shade of green.

Shriek of a monkey.

Bogart   God dammit.

Betty   There she is.

Jack   Good Lord.

Bogart   Where?

Jack   Do you see?

Bogart   Is it hanging or swinging?

Jack   It's crouching.

Betty   It's getting ready to jump.

Bogart   This just ain't natural; it should be behind bars.

Betty   I think it's a teensy bit unmanly for a man to be afraid of anything smaller than he is.

Bogart   It doesn't take a bear to kill a man.

Betty   It takes more than a mosquito.

Bogart   Well, fruit face, that's where you'd be wrong.

Katharine   It's the flies I could do without.

Jack   Flies won't hurt you. Just stay out of the water. It's the snails you want to avoid.

Katharine   Huston wants me in the water.

Jack   Don't go in the water. By all accounts this shoot has already earned a mention in *The Lancet* medical journal.

Katharine   Are they sending drugs or keeping score?

Bogart   What wouldn't I do for two cubes of ice.

Betty   I love my life with you, my friend, but right now I hate your life. I'm on the next canoe out of here. Meanwhile; Katie? Can I utilise your divine dressing room on your lovely little wooden raft?

Katharine   Of course.

Betty   I'm going to take a nap.

Bogart   Play another hand?

Betty   I said I need a nap.

Bogart   One more hand.

Betty   I need the kind of nap I need help with.

Bogart   That's quite enough information, baby. I'm playing one more hand.

Betty   When you do decide to come, beware of the monkeys and the bears and the snails. Especially the snails.

Bogart   I will. Thank you.

Betty *steps off the boat on to the raft and disappears.* **Jack** *and* **Bogart** *play cards.*

Bogart   There's something I need to know. I'm aware you're an English gentleman.

Jack   That's very nice of you to say so.

Bogart   Too damn English, too cautious with the key light.

Jack   No one complains.

Bogart   I'm complaining. I worked very hard to achieve this face. I don't want you ironing it out.

Jack   Too much debauchery there. You got me beat.

Bogart   When it comes to shooting you're as nancy as the rest of them, but your reputation off set goes before you. Your reputation as a man, I mean.

Jack   Ah; that reputation.

Bogart   Well, man to man; there is something you have to tell me.

Jack   What's that?

Bogart   Did you screw Marlene?

Jack   I couldn't possibly comment.

Katharine   Boys, oh you boys, you will not shock me with your manly confidences. Into either confrontation – Bogie; or submission – Jack.

Bogart   Put your fingers in your ears. Well?

Jack   I couldn't possibly comment.

Bogart   Considering the question I'd consider that a no.

Jack   If I didn't, it's because I'm a gentleman. If I did, it's because I was a gentleman. If I remain silent on the subject it's because I remain a gentleman.

Katharine   Bravo.

Bogart   Point taken.

Katharine   Bogie's the closest we come to a gentleman on the West Coast, but Jack, you out-class him with ease.

Bogart   You haven't heard the stories.

Katharine   Oh, but I have.

Bogart   I'll raise you ten.

Betty (*off*)   He's bluffing. Go all in. And hurry it up.

Bogart   When she's sleeping she doesn't like not to be disturbed. I'm not bluffing.

Jack   No? I *am* bluffing.

Bogart   You *are* a gentleman.

He rises, crosses.

Katharine   Monkey!

Bogart (*spins around*)   Where?

Katharine   Waaaaay over there.

Bogart   No wonder Spencer drinks.

He leaves.

Katharine   You're quiet today, Jack.

Jack   I'm wearing my poker face.

Katharine   Is that what you wore when you beat Marlene?

Jack   Who told you that?

Katharine   She did. Strip poker with the DOP. Well of course she'd lose.

Jack   You know, if you do swim in that I'll have to pry the leeches off you.

Katharine   I'd suffer leeches over your prying fingers any day. Sorry to disappoint. I'm sure Marlene didn't, if you did.

Jack   It doesn't count on location.

Katharine   Well, I don't wish to be counted, let alone not counted.

Jack   No one's counting.

Katharine   Do you think I'm frigid, Jack? They say I'm frigid.

Jack   I'm sure you're just . . . discriminating.

Katharine   Do you think I'm a lesbian, Jack? Some say I'm a lesbian.

Jack   Do you like girls?

Katharine   Oh, could you imagine? No, don't. I'm sure you could, so don't. I've never been tempted to stumble and fumble over my fellow stars, all that celebrity clambering. They are very tedious; the erotic aristocracy. You're Painter to the Court; don't you find them so?

Jack   I find they divide into those who somehow think they earned it and those who know their luck.

Katharine   The best of us stay deeply ordinary in a way, don't you find?

Jack   Yes, I have found that.

Katharine   Tell me you loved at least one of them.

Jack   I really haven't *had* that many.

Katharine   I don't want numbers. I don't even want names.
I want to know you've loved someone.

Jack   Yes.

Katharine   What was her name?

Jack   I loved Sophia.

Katharine   Really. You did?

Jack   You're surprised.

Katharine   Did she reciprocate?

Jack   I think so.

Katharine   My.

Jack   You're even more surprised.

Katharine   She seems a very . . . exotic choice for you, Jack.
You're the least Mediterranean person I know. What do you
think she saw in you?

Jack   I've really no idea. I suppose, perhaps; most men
know they need to flatter women, and most women smell the
bull-crap.

Katharine   Ah, that sweet scent of bull.

Jack   But it's my job to flatter women, it's my art, and there's
no bull-crap about it. It has to be the real thing. I suppose that
impresses them.

Katharine   And you're funny. And you're endearing.

Jack   Well, if you say so.

Katharine   Oh, you know you are. I'm admitting it because
I've seen you see me feeling it. You're also as transparent as a
glass vase and I know you have come to the opinion that I am
deeply fond of you. I've seen that look of bashful satisfaction
in your eyes. And I suspect you have it in mind, before this
shoot finishes, on some picturesque plain with wildebeest and

the odd giraffe, or after it's finished, on a single prop plane out of here with my fingernails pressed into your equally sweaty palm, that you will propose to me. If you were to do so I would be genuinely flattered and briefly silenced. I would be extremely polite, but you would sense an immediate reluctance. After a few platitudes I would decline. Quite firmly. I believe in economy, both verbal and emotional. I hope I haven't offended you.

Jack   No. But I must admit, it had crossed my mind.

Katharine   It had taken root, like a dandelion. One puff of wind and we'd be knee deep in weeds. I can see I've taken the wind out of your sails.

Jack   I'm not sure I had any wind in my sails. There was a light breeze, certainly. I was feeling the breeze, and yes, I suppose I had a sail up. But it was barely billowing.

Katharine   Well, it was about to billow, and take us scudding into mid-ocean. Please don't sulk.

Jack   I'm trying to think of something eloquent to say, but you set a high bar for eloquence. Whatever I say, you've already articulated and dismissed it. What I will say is, that in the process of dismissing it I feel you've also diminished it. I do indeed have feelings for you. Genuine feelings.

Katharine   Smell that aroma?

Jack   Feelings that run deeper than you think. If that has a whiff about it beware; because the crap might belong to that bull you've been fluttering your little red flag at.

Katharine   Well, touché, or am I mixing metaphors?

Jack   We look at one another.

Katharine   Yes, we do.

Jack   When things are at their most insane . . . we look at each other.

Katharine   We do indeed.

Jack   Sometimes we smile.

Katharine   Not always.

Jack   But sometimes. And one or other of us might arch an eyebrow.

Katharine   Oh yes; we might.

Jack   Well then.

Katharine   If that's why you want to marry me, it's a rather ephemeral reason.

Jack   A look from you is not an ephemeral thing.

Katharine   No, it isn't. But I didn't mean to light a flame.

Jack   But you saw a flame, and you fanned it.

Katharine   Yes, I did, didn't I?

Jack   Yes, you did.

Katharine   And I apologise.

Jack   And I do love you.

Pause.

Will Spencer ever marry you?

Katharine   Oh, I doubt it. I've no idea what I see in him. Except I find when I'm with him there's nothing else I wish to see. So for a few years yet I shall drag him out of the mean bar for which he has abandoned me on Thanksgiving. We shall kiss and make up for the very last time, and time and time again. I'm taken, Jack. Heart, head and soul. His shoulder is a rock, his feet are earth and his face is heaven. So whatever this world throws at us, the one of us will be there when the other succumbs to the grave. True love is the posy we've already left on one another's resting place. So. Do you have your answer, Jack?

Jack   I do.

Katharine Then quench your flame, Mr Englishman. Collapse that sail. Drag that shallow-breathing bull out of the arena.

Bogie *runs on with a medical manual. Distant thunder, maybe lightning.*

Bogart The flies!

Katharine What about them?

Bogart Listen to this. LISTEN TO THIS. 'Onchocerciasis infects 26 million people living near the rivers of sub-Saharan Africa.' That's here. That's a river. 'The disease is transmitted by the Simulium black fly which carries a larval form of the *filarial parasitic worm* Onchocerca volvulus. Larvae enter the skin at the site of the bite and the females release millions of microscopic *larvae* into the surrounding tissue.'

Katharine This doesn't end well, does it?

Jack 'When the larvae die, they cause skin rashes, depigmentation, and itchy nodules.'

Katharine How splendid.

Bogart Wait for it. 'A condition known as River Blindness can also occur.'

Katharine Oh, good Lord.

Bogart 'Half a million of those infected have been rendered *permanently blind*'!

Jack BLIND?!

Thunder. The monsoon stirs up and thrashes down.

Bogart I thought you'd appreciate that bit.

Jack Jesus H. Christ! Did Huston not research this hell-hole?

Bogart He just kept going up river until he found it.

Jack   The man's a lunatic. An irresponsible fucking cowboy!
I was willing to sacrifice every last comfort; my well-being and
my health. But my *sight*? Fuck him!

Katharine *grabs the book. The monsoon squalls.*

Jack   What do they look like?

Katharine   They look just like flies.

Jack   They must have some . . . distinguishing feature.

Bogart   Problem is, Jack; no one who's been bitten . . . has
ever been able to see one.

Jack   That is not funny.

Katharine   Jack, you're English. Surely you have some
natural immunity.

Jack   That is not bloody funny!

The tarpaulin comes loose.

Bogart   Jesus H. Christ! Get under cover.

He ushers **Katherine** *off. The scene transforms . . .*

Jack   We're surrounded by flies. I've been covered in flies.
I've got flies in my hair! I swallow a dozen of the damn things
with every martini! Damn you, Huston! You're no philosopher;
you're a fucking psychopath!

*He tears off his jacket. Uses it to whack at flies and mosquitos. During
his panic the scene transforms.*

I've risked falling into volcanoes and out of aeroplanes! I've
risked snake bites and dysentery. I will not risk my sight! You
little bastards! I DON'T WANT TO GO BLIND!

The thunder and rain stop. **Jack** *is suddenly still. The lights change. He
is back in the garage, but there is less of it. The artworks can still be seen,
hanging in the void.*

Jack   Why is it so dark in here?

The door opens. **Marilyn Monroe** *comes in.*

Marilyn I'm late. I know. I'm sorry.

Jack Never you mind.

Marilyn My mother said I was to apologise if I was even five minutes late. I spend most of my life apologising. It's not that I'm deliberately late, it's just that I get to a place and discover I am?

Jack I was happy to wait.

Marilyn Some are, some aren't.

Jack May I say, you are looking utterly enchanting.

Marilyn You're a gentleman, I know. And a liar.

Jack It's true.

Marilyn I look atrocious.

Jack Luminous.

Marilyn Sure. And I put so much effort into it. How are you today, Jack?

Jack We had a little something planned.

Marilyn Did we?

Jack You know we did.

He moves to his 'Vermeer'.

I was standing in front of this, the original, the day I became *conscious* of light.

He moves from the 'Vermeer' to the 'Van Gogh'.

And when I stumbled in front of this for the first time the light poured *through* my eyes and and came to life inside my head.

He moves to his own stuff.

I still shuffled about like the Vaudevillian's child I am, but my eyes were open to an elevated realm; Shiva's swirling realm of photon. Under that green canopy, on the excavated walls of

Troy, at the ballet, in the desert, on the village green; even amidst the garish surround of my petty, pretty artifice . . . light has been my life. And you are made of it, and I shall capture it. Chiaroscuro is too harsh for you. A soft enveloping light is what we need. A low key-light and a very gentle fill.

Marilyn   I'm sure I don't know what you are talking about.

Jack   You promised.

Marilyn   Yes, but if I did it was only to please you.

Jack   Then please me.

Marilyn   Well, as long as you expect nothing of me. I have nothing to give. I shall just sit here like a lemon without a thought in my head.

Jack   So be it. I found a hat for you to wear.

Marilyn   I don't wear hats. I look like an ice-cream sundae.

Jack   You'll like this hat.

Marilyn   I won't.

Jack   You will. This is the hat.

Marilyn   I love it.

He sets up lights, and his vintage Hasselblad.

Jack   I've had this beauty for twenty years.

Marilyn   I hate my nose.

Jack   I know you do.

Marilyn   How did you know?

Jack   You touch it a lot.

Marilyn   I do not.

Jack   Well, yes you do.

Marilyn   I do? Do I?

Jack   Yes.

Marilyn   You think I'm hiding something?

Jack   You've nothing to hide. You are exquisite.

Marilyn   Yeah. That's how I get through the day.

Jack   Incandescent.

Marilyn   Like a moth.

Jack   Lie back a little.

Marilyn   My favourite position. I didn't mean that the way it came out.

Jack   The thing about a hat –

Marilyn   I don't wear hats.

Jack   It's not enough to put it on. You have to *wear* the hat.

Marilyn   Could you hide my nose with the hat?

Jack   The key light that suits you most is lower than usual.

Marilyn   I'll bet you say that to all the girls.

Jack   It accentuates your nose.

Marilyn   Oh God, I *hate* my nose.

Jack   Thus the angle of the inky-dink.

Marilyn   The inky-dink?

Jack   The lamp.

Marilyn   I see.

Jack *takes a photograph.*

Marilyn   I wasn't ready.

Jack   That's why I took it.

Marilyn   Oh.

He takes another.

Jack   So. Were you looking at the camera or was the camera looking at you?

Marilyn   Which is best?

Jack   Both are good. But you have to choose. You try to do both at once, and that's not possible.

Marilyn   You're right. That's what I do.

Jack   You must leave the moment to me. Don't try to shape the moment. I will shape the moment. All you have to be . . . is in it.

They are very close. **Arthur Miller** *has entered through the smaller door, and is watching.*

Arthur   I wouldn't entirely trust him, if I were you.

Marilyn   Jack wants to immortalise me.

Arthur   I'm sure that's not all he wants.

Jack   Don't jump to conclusions, my dear fellow. Art is an intimate thing.

Arthur   I'm very well aware of that.

Jack   We shall both attempt to immortalise her, but between you and I, she needs no help from either of us.

Arthur   Obfuscate all you like. You have this woman stretched out on a chaise . . .

Marilyn   He was taking my photograph, that's all he was doing.

Jack   I wouldn't trust her either, Arthur, but I'm a gentleman. I'd keep your powder dry if I were you.

Katharine *appears with a mailing box in hand.*

Katharine   I saw you from the window, sneaking in.

Jack   Katie! What are you doing here?

Katharine   You think you're going to take him to the pub.

Jack   Is he? Jolly good. Bury the hatchet.

Katharine   Well, you're not taking him to the pub.

Jack   Is he not? Are you at Pinewood?

Katharine   I'm your wife, Jack, and I've got something for you. It was just delivered.

Arthur   I didn't come here to take him to the pub.

Jack   He came to punch me on the nose.

Arthur   I just dropped by to see how the book was going.

Jack   He thinks I was attempting to seduce his wife.

Katharine   And what about Jack? How's Jack?

Jack   Spiffing, thanks.

Arthur   Of course, how's Jack?

Jack   On top of the – round thing with green bits and blue bits.

Marilyn   The world.

Jack   The world. And I *was* attempting to seduce his wife.

Marilyn   I'm not his wife!

Jack   Don't talk bloody nonsense.

Katharine   Not as easy as it looks, is it?

Jack   And you're not even on this one! You're on the wrong bloody sound stage!

Arthur   For Christ's sake, just settle down!

Jack (*suddenly aggressive*)   Would you like to punch me on the nose?

Arthur   No, thank you.

Katharine   Jack!

Jack   Would fisticuffs with the Englishman assuage your displeasure?

Arthur   Would they assuage your guilt?

Jack   I *adore* your wife! You don't deserve her, you pretentious scribbler! She's beyond exquisite!

He grabs **Marilyn** *and gives her a Technicolor kiss.*

Katharine   Jack, no!

Arthur   Steady on, now!

Jack   Take your best shot. Put one right there.

Katharine   Jack!

Jack   I sparred with Huston. Gave Hitchcock a piece of my mind. Told Rambo to go fuck himself.

Arthur   You're a man to be reckoned with.

Jack   Correct!

He punches **Arthur** *on the chin.*

Marilyn   Oh.

Katharine   No, Jack! No.

Jack   Ow.

Katharine   Stop it now.

Jack   I'm Jack Cardiff!

Katharine   Yes. Yes you are. And look. This is for you.

Jack   Who?

Katharine   Look, Jack. Look and see.

She opens the mailing box. **Jack** *looks in the box and takes out a prism. It has a profound effect on him.*

Katharine   It's a prism.

Jack   Not possible.

Katharine   Why not?

Jack   It got broken.

Katharine   It's another.

Jack   It's a prism.

Katharine   Yes.

Jack *holds it up to the light. The prism refracts an extravagant rainbow.*

Jack   Hold on a minute. Déjà vu.

Blackout.

Scene Two

Jack *is studying a small 'Renoir'. He has a small palette of oils and a brush in his hand.* **Nicola** *comes in.*

Nicola   Jack?

Jack   Hmm?

Nicola   What's that?

Jack   It's my Renoir.

Nicola   You copied that? I didn't know.

Jack   Her eyebrow's wrong. Thanks for the porridge.

Nicola   My pleasure.

Jack   It tasted like rheumatism.

Nicola   Do you know what day it is?

Jack   Well, I've one chance in seven.

Nicola   It's your birthday.

Jack   Ah. One chance in three hundred and sixty-five.

Nicola   Do you know how old you are?

Jack   One in a thousand. Feels like. The younger you say, the older I'll feel. Will there be cake?

Nicola   Yes. You can have some if you tell me one thing.

Jack   What's that?

Nicola   Who am I, Jack?

Jack   Is this a trick question?

Nicola   No cake if you don't answer.

Jack   Do I have to answer *correctly*?

Nicola   It would be nice if you could.

Pause. **Jack** *tries to answer, but doesn't know who she is. He grins and goes back to his painting.*

Nicola   When I'm not her, I'm faceless, aren't I? You used to tell me I had 'a good heart', well, it's broken now. The first time you didn't know me it broke in two, and Katie crawled out of it.

Jack   Katie! Just a small slice.

Nicola   Sophia – so what. Marlene – so be it. Marilyn . . . I could never quite tell. She brought out the gentlemen in most of them; she may have tempted the devil in you. The rest: who cares. But when you speak of Katharine, she's there between us, a butterfly woken by a midwinter fire. I think it was her, not I, who found the true man in you. I'm good at denial, because for thirty years I could reach out and touch you, which she could not. But now I need to *know*, Jack. Because if Katie was the love of your life, that means I was not.

Pause. **Jack** *beams at her. Happy to be in her company, but clueless as to what she's talking about.*

Nicola   I haven't her wit or her wisdom. Her worldliness, I know. Damn you, Jack; I was never any of those things. I was a cute little urchin. I willed myself to be gamine and chic for you. If you *had* to replace me with someone, could it not, for the love of heaven, have been *Audrey*.

Pause.

Jack   What was the question again?

Nicola   I'll get the cake.

Lucy *enters.*

Lucy   Hi.

Nicola   Hello.

Lucy   Hello Jack.

He doesn't know her.

Jack   . . . Hello.

He returns to his painting.

Lucy   He seems happy.

Nicola   He's further from us.

Lucy   He's calm when you're here.

Nicola   Have we had any more little incidents?

Lucy   No, none at all. It was only the once.

Nicola   You presume to understand Jack's symptoms better than I, so you were perfectly aware that impulsive behaviour and a lack of inhibition were to be expected. Which is the best reason I can imagine for not encouraging them.

Lucy   It was a mistake; I'm sorry.

Nicola   I've been half inclined to let you go.

Lucy   No, please.

Nicola   If I ever think that would be best for Jack, I shall.

Lucy   Please don't.

Nicola   Then let's continue on more of an even keel, shall we?

She leaves.

Lucy   Happy birthday, Jack.

Jack   Thank you.

Lucy   This is for you.

Jack   Thank you. Put it under the tree.

Lucy   OK.

She puts the parcel aside.

Ask me what I did last night? Jack? I watched *The Red Shoes*. There were colours I'd never seen before. So I watched it again. I watched *The Red Shoes* all bloody night. I hate unhappy endings; but damn your eyes, Jack. I loved *The Red Shoes*.

Jack   I'm not sure I've seen that one.

Lucy   If anyone asks, please tell them you need me. You wouldn't want to lose me, would you, Jack?

Jack   I've lost a few people lately.

Lucy   I've lost my little girl.

Jack   What little girl?

Lucy   Beatrice. Little Bee. They took her from me.

Jack   Who did?

Lucy   They said I was incapable, of providing proper care.

Jack   They took her where?

Lucy   I stand outside the nursery on the days I'm not to see her. I watch her through the gate. It's not a Tuesday or a Friday so I don't speak to her. I mustn't touch her. I just stand there hoping that on Friday she remembers who I am.

Jack   Who does?

Lucy   I need to show them that I'm sorted. Don't let Nikki get rid of me, Jack. I know I'm not up to much. But I've tried. I've tried to be whatever you want me to be.

Jack *looks at her quizzically, then suddenly gets up and goes into the bathroom. Comes out having unpegged a slightly damp 8 x 10 photograph. She looks at it.*

Jack   Like it?

Lucy   I don't look like this.

Jack   It's a fair likeness

Lucy   If only.

Jack   If only?

Lucy   If only I could be the way you see me.

Mason *opens the door and* **Nicola** *enters with a modest birthday cake.*

Nicola
    Happy Birthday to you.

Mason/Nicola
    Happy Birthday to you.

Mason/Nicola/Lucy
    Happy Birthday dear Jack,
    Happy Birthday to you.

Jack   Well that's cleared up any confusion. Quite obviously, I'm five years old.

He goes back to his painting.

Nicola   Blow the candle out and make a wish.

Jack   I wish you'd all fuck off and leave me in peace. Hang me in a tree, dump me on the ice.

Nicola   Please, don't talk like that.

She blows out the candle. He turns round the painting.

Jack   Finished. What do you think?

Nicola   It's good, Jack.

Lucy   It's pretty.

Nicola   It's luscious.

Mason   You'd be hard pressed to tell it from the original.

Nicola   You were distraught when you had to sell it; remember?

Jack   Didn't have the heart. I just cancelled the insurance. Hid it in a box under the bed.

Mason   But this is a copy.

Jack   No; it's the original.

Mason   No; it's a copy. There's wet paint.

Jack   I was never happy with her eyebrow.

Mason   Jesus H. Christ.

Jack   Much improved. Wouldn't you say so?

Nicola   Oh dear Lord.

Mason   Fu . . . cking hell.

Jack   About time it saw the light of day. We'll hang it in the house.

Nicola   Yes. Let's.

Mason   Unfuckingbelievable.

Nicola   It doesn't look too bad.

Mason (*to* **Lucy**)   You're supposed to be keeping an eye on him.

Lucy   You said to keep him occupied.

Mason   Writing! Not desecrating priceless fucking masterpieces!

Nicola   Mason! We'll just let it dry.

She blows on it.

Mason   Let it dry? Has he written a single bloody sentence lately?

Nicola   Mason, not today.

Mason   Have you put pen to paper at all in the last month?

Jack   'You've lived a hell of a life, Jack. Get it down on paper, Jack.' Christ; I can't remember what I had for breakfast!

Mason   You wrecked a Renoir for breakfast!

Jack   Living this life I can just about tolerate, but reliving it is doing my fucking head in. Rheumatism!

Mason   I would like us all, to the best of our varying abilities, to acknowledge that there is a great deal of interest in this. Jonty's managed to get to Scorsese. I'm telling you now. If you finish this thing, Scorsese will write the foreword.

Jack   Best of his generation. Never bloody checked me.

Mason   You are letting a great opportunity pass you by.

Nicola   Yes, but whose?

Jack   Nose to the old, um . . . *Flintstones* . . . car was a log, wheels were a thing . . .

Lucy   Grindstone.

Jack   Grindstone! Just end up with a bloody nose.

Mason   Scorsese, for fuck's sake. It could lead to great things.

Nicola   Not for Jack. It won't make an iota of difference to Jack.

Jack   Exactly! What's an iota?

Mason   Dad; there could be a film in this.

Nicola   And there's the thing.

Jack   I made a great many, you know. I directed a few.

Mason   You directed fourteen.

Jack   Three very fine films. Eleven piss-poor ones.

Mason   And why was that?

Jack   Because all they would give me was shite. Photograph something decent, or direct this turkey. Christ, I shot some rubbish. Don't hang on to the end of my shirt tail or you'll find yourself mired in the same crap they dragged me through. Beware ambition.

Mason   I'm aware you despise my aspirations, but I don't want to be an operator until the day I die.

Nicola   You became an operator to emulate him. You wanted to emulate him because you adored him. Where's that gone? Why have you forgotten that?

Mason   I've lived in his shadow my entire working life. Shunted off to boarding school, ignored in the studio canteen, crawling up from clapper loader, stuck operating for decades, never trusted, never lauded. Tolerated. Nevertheless, I'm doing this for him.

Nicola   Your father's ill, so suddenly this industry of pirates becomes compassionate. Well, it's a fake compassion and it won't spread to you.

Mason   That's uncalled for.

Nicola   What Jack's got can't be passed to someone else like an Olympic flame outside a sweetshop in Hillingdon. It's his. Not yours!

Mason   I'm just trying to bring his life to a meaningful conclusion.

Pause.

Nicola   Oh, Mason.

Jack   There is no need for you to concern yourself with my mortality, thank you very much. And my sodding immortality is none of your bloody business, either. I'm not going to write a bloody book!

Nicola   Can we please forget about the book.

Mason   Forgotten.

Pause.

Jack   What book's that then?

Nicola   Was that a joke?

Jack   Do you know; I think it was.

Lucy   You've written it.

Jack   Written what?

Lucy   Your book. More or less.

Jack   No, that I would remember.

Lucy   No, that's what you keep forgetting.

She finds the package she gave him earlier.

Lucy   I've found pages all over the place – in drawers, that trunk. Quite a pile of it in that old case you brought in from the house. And there was more on the tape. I've transcribed most of it. It'll need properly organising, but there's more than enough of it. There's even an ending; I found an 'End'. You'd scribbled it at the bottom of a page.

Jack   Good God.

Lucy   Happy Birthday, Jack.

Mason   You devious bastard.

Jack   Who wrote this?

Lucy   You wrote this.

Jack   Is this all me?

Lucy   Yes.

Jack   Well, what the fucking hell have you all had me doing for the last four months!

Mason   You've deliberately squirreled that away!

Jack   Is it up to snuff?

Lucy   Yes, I think so.

Jack   Feels heavy for a book, but rather light for a life.

He peers at the pages.

Is it especially dark in here?

Lucy   Not really.

Nicola   It could be brighter.

Jack   I'd rather not read it now.

Nicola   No.

Jack   That would mean suffering it a third bloody time. Do you see?

Nicola *takes the book and gives it to* **Mason**.

Jack   Not a patch on your stuff, Arthur.

Mason   You know very well who I am.

Jack   Ha ha. Remember when we stood on the walls of the palace at Mycenae? Looked across the desert. Saw chariots, and armies in the sand . . . Agamemnon with his trophy of war, his mistress, his Cassandra. His wife Clytemnestra at the gate who, quite reasonably, went on to kill the both of them with an axe. That's the picture we should make. Nepotism aside, boy; you're a decent operator.

Mason   Thank you.

Jack   Look after this.

He offers **Mason** *the prism, then changes his mind.*

Jack   Second thoughts; you're a clumsy sod. This is priceless.

He tries to look through it, tries to conjure colours.

Jack   You know; it is dark in here. You need a bit of sunlight through these things. I'm going to sit in the sun. What there is of it.

Lucy   I'll put your chair out.

*She helps **Jack** out into the sunshine and opens up a folding picnic chair. **Jack** sits there, playing with his prism.*

Mason   Where on earth did you find one of those?

Nicola   The Museum in Bradford. They had two. I said the magic words: Jack Cardiff.

Mason   A 'decent operator'. I've always been virtually invisible.

Nicola   You're not the only one who's disappeared. I've lived half my life through that man's eyes, and he can't see me any more. An impossible love he once felt has completely erased me. He threw in his hand with me. Not because he'd found his prize, but because the fairground lights were going out. I have always been . . . his consolation.

Jack   Something's not right with this bloody thing. It's misaligned, or Japanese.

Nicola   Something's wrong with him today.

Mason   I'm getting this published.

Lucy   I think he's content.

Mason   He's hanging over an abyss and you two are waving. I'm not letting go so easily.

Lucy   He's over there, Mason.

Mason   I know.

He sits and delves into the manuscript.

Lucy   I don't mean to take liberties. It's what I thought you wanted.

Nicola   You can't put a life on paper, or on celluloid. We are written on time. Not even in ink; we are pencilled in. We are a light pencil, for a while. We make some appointments, we keep a few, we are torn out and crumpled up and thrown to the wind. We disappear.

Jack
  Red, and yellow, and pink and green.
  Orange and purple and . . .

What a bloody terrible song that is.

Nicola   Mason was rude to you. And I've been less than pleasant. I'm sorry.

Lucy   That's OK.

Nicola   I think you're doing a very fine job with Jack.

Lucy   Thank you.

Nicola   I think you love him a little. And I thank you for that.

Lucy   It's not difficult. I like working here. I never know who I'm going to be.

Nicola   There's a room in the house. It's a big house. There's a room there, if that would be convenient for you.

Lucy   Thank you. Yes it would.

Nicola   Put things on a more permanent footing.

Lucy   Yes.

Jack *comes inside with the prism.*

Jack   Worse than useless, of course. Camera's obsolescent. They don't make the stock any more. The Rolls-Royce is stuck in the garage. Its owner's still behind the wheel, with a silk cravat and a rictus grin.

Avengers *theme again,*

Bombom-bombom-bombom-bombombom. Who gave me this?

Nicola   I did.

Jack   I love it. It's absolutely my favourite thing.

Nicola   I'm glad.

He peers at her through the prism, turning it a little.

Jack   It's got two miniature yous in it. A cyan Katie . . . Oh, and a magenta Nicola. How about that?

Nicola   Hello, Jack.

Jack   Hello, Nikki. Are you in love with anybody? No. No; don't answer that. I could love a woman like you.

Nicola   I could love a man like you, Jack.

Jack   I love you, Nikki. You're life and I'm leaving you.

He sits.

Mason   Dad? This is well written.

Jack   What do you know, Bogart? You only read your own bits.

Mason *gives him a steady look.*

Mason   It's very good.

Jack   Reliving past glory is not a comfortable thing, you know. It reminds you more of the past than the glory.

Mason   'It would be far more conducive growing old gracefully if our lives were lived in a rewarding and heartening sequence. Submit your life to any decent script editor and they'd reject it on structure alone.'

Jack   A real life does not boast a satisfying story arc. We are doomed to live the events of our lives in the wrong damn order; it's like shooting a film, not watching one. The time of our lives . . .

Mason   'The time of our lives is not the finished masterpiece; it's just whatever we got in the can today. today.'

Jack   I'd say that's a wrap; and the sun is well over the yardarm.

Mason   Scotch and soda?

Jack   I'd love one.

Lucy   He said your name.

Nicola   He did. Unfortunately the dialogue was from *A Matter of Life and Death*.

Jack   A hopeless third act but a very happy ending.

Nicola   If you say so, Jack.

Jack   I did not choose this. I would be otherwise.

Nicola   I know.

Jack *looks at watch. He's not wearing one.*

Jack   If I were on location I'd have them rushing around like mad things right about now. Magic hour's a misnomer; it's more like a magic minute.

Lucy   What is?

Jack   The hour's what you need to prepare for the minute. Another fucking life metaphor. Give me that scotch so I can rinse my bloody mouth out.

Lucy *holds out the scotch.* **Jack** *holds out his hand in a completely wrong direction. Her surprise as their hands hang suspended. Then she moves the glass to his hand. He smiles and takes it. Her hand lingers for a moment in front of his eyes, and her fingers dance. He takes no notice. He sips.*

He is entirely blind. He moves his glass to the table, **Lucy** *slides the table beneath the glass just in time.*

He gazes ahead.

Jack   Look at that. People think it's about the gold of the
sunset, but it's not. It's the under-exposure from the sinking
sun forces the sky to that stunning deep blue. Look at it. That's
worth scheduling an entire day around. I've worked half my
life around it. Just look at it. Lighting by God. Look at it. Look.

Lucy   Yes. I see it. I can see.

Light transforms their surroundings.

Jack   It'll be dark soon. Good moon tonight, for all the good
that'll do us. I love the moonlight. It's always been a tragedy to
me, that we cannot shoot the moon. Day for Night makes me
wince although when it comes to Day for Night I'm the damn
champion. If only we could shoot the moonlight. We're going
to need a fifty K and we're going to need it high. They don't
build a cherry-picker high enough. We're going to put it on
that cliff. And Bogie, I have an idea. Phosphorescence. You
remember last night – the way the shallows glowed? Since
the dawn of time the world has burned with such inventive
luminosity. Well, dammit; we do just one day for night shot;
just their feet through the shallows. If I shoot against the sun
I'll catch the sparkle. With no red in the filter and I pull it right
down in post; more green than blue; you've got phosphorescence.
I'm gonna outwit Double Ugly. I'm gonna make him write a
line. Then; and this is it. We've the fifty K for moonlight but
we track a red head with a turquoise filter from a low angle;
throw it off a mirror. I'm going to recreate that remarkable
light that laps at our feet. I'm going to capture that on Katie's
chin. Katie's gonna squeal but when she sees the result she'll
love it. Bogie?

Mason   Yes, Jack.

Jack   What do you think?

Mason   It's a great idea.

Jack   You see the cliff?

Mason   Of course. Who could miss it?

Jack   Can you get the boys up there?

Mason   By hook or by crook.

Jack   Mason, we should have shot together years ago. My life on film; who'd have thought it. Only you could have pulled this off, my son. You've done a tremendous job, my boy. A tremendous job.

Mason   Thank you.

Jack   Now look. Magic hour draws to a close. Not enough to shoot in any more and the sun's halfway over the horizon. Next little treat is the green flash. It's shootable; I've shot it; it's a strange inversion from orange to green, lasts not even a second. It's like the olive on top of a pink martini. Watch for it.

Mason   Yes.

Jack   Don't take your eyes off it. Look at it.

Mason   I'm looking.

Jack   So much to see. I sometimes think I'm the luckiest man in the world.

Nicola   We're lucky to have you, Jack.

Jack   Look, Katie; the basher boys are on the cliff, making moonlight for you. And look at your feet. Look at the water. A billion dancing particles of living light.

Nicola   I'm looking.

Jack   Yes, but *look*. No, look at the sun; there it goes, wait for the flash.

Light transforms to the embers of sunset.

There it was. Did you see it?

Nicola   Yes, I saw it.

She has taken his hand.

Jack

> The girl I love is up in the gallery
> The girl I love is looking now at me
> There she is, can't you see, waving her handkerchief
> As merry as a robin that sings in a tree.

Mason *touches his shoulder, and* **Jack** *grips his hand. They stare ahead.* **Nicola** *has no need of a menthol stick; her tears fall freely.*

Jack   Just look at that. Look at it.

End.

Ken

Ken was first staged at Hampstead Theatre Downstairs, London, on 7 April 2016, with the following cast:

The Writer   Terry Johnson
Ken   Jeremy Stockwell

Writer   Terry Johnson
Director   Lisa Spirling
Designer   Janet Bird
Lighting Designer   Mike Gunning
Sound Designer   John Leonard

Characters

The Writer *is rigid: he stands at a lectern, or sits at a desk, or his shoes are nailed to the floor.*

Ken *is free to wander: he begins the show in the audience. Utilising unexpected properties and costume, he also embodies some of the other characters.*

Note

The Writer's dialogue is in regular type.

Ken's dialogue is in this sans-serif type.

Prologue

Once upon a time, just outside Manchester, they built a Pleasure Palace and a zoological garden and they called it Bellevue. By the time I discovered it the ballroom was derelict, the attractions and the pleasures were all long gone. To gain access to the zoo one had to squeeze through a rupture in a chain-link fence beyond which the enclosures stood, rusted, overgrown and empty. The animals were gone; lost in the memories of children long grown up, but their cages now accessible, though trepidatious to enter. The ghost of a lion is the least settled of ghosts.

What I'm about to tell you is not entirely true. Telling the unadulterated truth rarely achieves a tale that is true to the bone. So I make no apology for my inaccuracies of memory, nor my wilful perversions of it, because, firstly, the lies are all small and white; and secondly, the things you doubt, the utterances you least believe, are without exception the things most likely to be true.

One

I was twenty-three years old but I knew nothing of the magical qualities associated with that number. I was no numerologist. I did not perceive myself to be beneath the portal that divides the future from the past. I was merely twenty-three. It's where I was.

I was living behind a thin partition wall in a small flat near the North End Road: a sliver of a room with a bricked-up window courtesy of an ancient window tax, a sleeping space of tomb-like dimensions stolen from the living room where nightly, Maxine, Joe and various of their friends would meet, smoke dope, snort coke, chew dried fungus and drink Special Brew until four o'clock in the morning. I tended to retire at eleven or so, and the partition was only slightly thinner than my tolerance.

As far as I could discern it, the purpose of taking drugs seemed to be: to enable you to *talk* about the drugs you had just taken, or the drugs you once took, which were a) far superior to the ones you had just taken, or b) life-threatening. And to do so for hours on end.

And so I would retreat into my bricked-up, partitioned sliver of a room, sit at the chrome green Underwood typewriter that my mother had proudly gifted me, and continue my quest to write a play about a dead zoo.

Which is what I was doing when the telephone rang.

Hello?

It's Ken Campbell here. Is Jeff there?

Well, no. Jeff moved out. I think he's in Amsterdam.

Is he coming back?

I don't think so.

Oh. Who are you?

I'm Terry.

What do you do?

Well, I, er . . . at the moment I'm writing a play.

Is it any good?

I don't really know. It might be, eventually.

Is that all you do?

Well, I've done a bit of acting.

Excellent. What are you doing on Saturday?

Well, um . . .

I'm getting some people together on Saturday. If I were you I'd come.

Um, well, I wasn't really . . .

Can you do Welsh?

Welsh?

Can you sound like a Welshman?

Er, well . . . probably.

Go on then; speak to me like a Welshman.

(*Welsh dialect.*) I don't really know what to say.

Excellent. Irish?

(*Irish dialect.*) Well, I'm sure it wouldn't past muster in Dublin but I could give it a go.

Ha ha! Yorkshire.

(*Yorkshire dialect.*) Now, I *do* know Yorkshire. It's where complete strangers talk to you for no discernable reason.

Alright – you think you're clever. A South African Geordie.

Well in fact I might know how to do a South African! (*Jewish.*) You start like a North London Jew (*Australian.*) and you take him across to Australia and then you go back to the equator and once you're there you've (*South African.*) got a South African. (*Writer.*) If he was Geordie he'd have odd vowels as well, I suppose. He'd probably sound like . . . (*South African Geordie.*) a fairground gypsy with dodgy adenoids, chatting up girls on a waltzer.

Mm, well: that's very good! Jim Broadbent's fucked off; you've got his parts.

His parts in what?

See you on Saturday.

And on Saturday I trekked off to Haverstock Hill, deaf to the universe that had raised its megaphone to yell:

Come in Number 23, your time is nigh!

Entirely unaware, I was stepping through a rupture in the chain-link fence of my life. I was stepping through a portal. So important a portal it had christened itself . . .

The Warp.

The Warp! Ha ha!

Two

Ken Campbell was a short man with a Popeye swagger and a porkpie hat. He had the face of a friendly but permanently bewildered grocer. Baggy casual combat trousers designed for everyday philosophical conflicts in Hampstead village, a loose-knit sweater, as might be worn by a *Beano* character-turned-deep-sea fisherman, and a pair of those idiosyncratically constructed Birkenstock shoes which, inexplicably, are not the same shape as human feet.

And if history ordained that Dali was to be defined by his moustache, and Freud his beard, then Ken had most certainly bagsied the eyebrows.

Their growth encouraged by the energetic catalogue of facial expressions of which they were the most prominent feature, they caressed his forehead like two grey Victorian moustaches applied the wrong way up.

He opened the door with a baby over his shoulder and a small terrier shagging his left shin. The baby was very new and it was called Daisy. The dog was called Werner, named for Werner Ehart, the man who thought up EST, which was a seminar-based technique for releasing human potential. The seminars were very expensive, very trendy, and totally devoid of toilet breaks. If you paid for the full course you'd emerge with enough self-confidence to have everything you wanted whenever you wanted it.

Ken's dog had completed the course and was wholly confident in his pursuit of biscuits, tennis balls and warm shins.

Excuse the dog. Welcome! Who are you?

I'm Terry.

Excellent. I'm Ken.

But the trim of his eyebrows suggested a distinct disappointment in me. I was almost certainly dressed entirely in purple. Purple cotton flares, purple tongue-collar shirt and purple zip-up jumper. A studied attempt at individualisation by a young man who had donned blue jeans only once, and found it impossible to sit down in them. Purple seemed a suitably individual statement. *Entirely* purple seemed a suitably confident one. But not having done the EST course, my self-confidence was self-constructed and subsequently fragile. My hair was fashionably long, but quite inexplicably parted on the side. (My advice now to all young men as regards their hair is: listen to your father.)

I'm guessing you're the playwright. You certainly look like one. Come on in.

Ken's eyebrows perked up as he ushered me down the corridor.

There's a bunch of folk here. The ones I know are really terrific. The ones I don't know haven't made up their minds if they're going to be terrific or not. But they've made it thus far so there's a half-decent chance they'll turn out to be as terrific as the rest. This is them.

I entered the room. The bed on a raised mezzanine. The dining table inherited from parents in the Essex estuary. Motley, well-worn sofas, their sags and eccentricities disguised by third-world rugs and throws. A pink bicycle. A Punch and Judy booth. And the sickly sweet smell of burning joss-sticks masking the pungent whiff of smouldering weed. The assembled thespians, musicians, hangers-on, alternatives, hippies, chicks, dudes and children were arranged not on a single plane but on many levels; on cushions, low stools, tall stools, platforms, mattresses, a step ladder; people 'hanging out' from floor to ceiling.

This is Terry. He thinks he's a genius. This is everyone else worth knowing.

Hi.

Hi, Terry.

Hi.

Hello, Terry.

'Lo.

In one corner, cross-legged on a plush Indian cushion of multi-coloured felt, was John Joyce, the Irish character man. He was at least ten years too old for cross-legged cushion sitting, but he seemed stoically content. A scruffy, ruddy, slightly down-at-heel Buddha from Sligo. John had a round ruddy face and bright coal-black eyes. His hair is slicked into submission. I suspect he hoards a diminishing store of Brylcreem.

His eyebrows are aspirant eyebrows; they yearn to take on the aspect of Ken's, but in their hearts, the hairy heart of eyebrow, they know they never will. Which doesn't prevent them slyly flicking skywards when a touch of blarney passes his disturbingly kissable lips.

So: you've met Ken now, so you have.

There's an old adage about loyalty; the man who would set himself on fire and jump into a canal if the other feller asked him to? Well, John had felt that lick of flame, and the shocking chill of that canal. He was Ken's trusted lieutenant and had stuck and would stick with him through thick and thin. He grinned amiably, shifted up on his cushion, and patted it. I sat next to him.

So, you're a genius?

I don't think so. I didn't say I was.

Well, you see, you have the demeanour of a genius.

Do I?

You do; you look like one who doesn't know he is, yet. It's possibly the side parting. I can see by your face and the colour of your flares you think you're on a precipice. But you're not, you know. You're still in the foothills looking up. You think you daren't put your trust in strangers, but you must put your trust in the strangest of strangers. I know this; you see; I've a bit of the gypsy in me.

Ken interjects through the kitchen hatch.

You'll have to ignore John Joyce. I've told him he has to be Billy McGuinness until teatime. You can join in if you like, but he may be intuiting stuff it's a bit beyond him to intuit. On the other hand he is Irish, so he might hit on one or two nuggets; you never know.

John Joyce beamed, the benevolent glint of McGuinness in his eye.

I was handed a mug of thinly perfumed tea by the most beautiful woman I had ever seen. Her name was Mya.

Mya. Ha ha.

And after four decades she remains the most beautiful woman I have ever seen. She was wearing a flowing halter-necked dress of translucent chiffon with little beneath it.

It is a vision permanently etched in my memory, and one that I profoundly doubt, because I have no memories of Mya in which she is *not* wearing translucent chiffon with little beneath it. I shall re-dress her in a silken patchwork skirt to her ankles, and a pink angora sweater, though even then she remains an improbable presence in a reality deeply unworthy of her.

Hello, Terry.

Hello.

How old are you?

Twenty-three.

What's your date of birth?

Twenty, twelve, fifty-five.

Eighty-seven. That's a good number.

Mya was a numerologist.

Old restraints to be shed; lovely stuff ahead.

She dipped her head and continued on with her tray of Lapsang Souchon.

Across from me, lounging in a deep armchair, thin long legs tapering to a very good pair of brogues and crossed at the ankles, was a gaunt man in his early thirties. Russell had a pleasant face, which was smiling at me. A smile from a stranger that seemed to say; you may not know me, but I know you. I've known you for a long while. I recognise you from previous lives and a universe not entirely parallel to the one you currently inhabit. A silent greeting hinting at a cosmic welcome.

In the corner, a man with a cubist head, sockless, in sturdy black shoes, was studiously sketching. Mitch was a painter, and a damn good one. Hyper realism was his game, at least on canvas. For real life he chose a more expressionist technique. He was designing a poster for the forthcoming venture.

Eventually Ken defined the helm of the room by standing in it and announced . . . The Caper.

What it is, is . . . we shall Journey to the Centre of the Edinburgh Festival where the derelict Regal Cinema, a veritable palace of gigantic proportions has been secured for 150 quid. Due to its having no screen, no seats, and no toilets.

No safety certificates, no licenses, no heating. No electric.

Ha ha.

These unique qualifications for an entertainment venue had made it the natural choice in which for Ken to present what was to become his masterwork.

The Warp!

We would, in a mere ten days, refurbish the cinema, build a set of six stages in the stalls, plumb in some toilets, rehearse a play, and put it on. A not entirely impossible feat one might imagine, but for the fact that the chosen drama was of twenty-four hours duration.

Is there anyone here who can plumb in toilets?

I was somewhat reassured that this was the first item on the agenda; it at least suggested a rational approach. Foolishly volunteering that my father was a plumber I inadvertently volunteered myself.

Excellent; we have synchronicity in the bathroom department. The bogs are yours. You'll also be playing the mystic grocer, which is about the best part, so I think that's fair.

*

The genesis of *The Warp* is worthy of a place in the drama itself. Ken was a determined collector of all things out of the ordinary. His cry of . . .

Good evening, Seekers!

. . . had propelled the likes of Bob Hoskins and Sylvester McCoy to the pinnacles of stardom in pubs and theatre car parks up and down the country. His anarchic *Roadshow* had introduced an unsuspecting audience to his particularly skewed yet optimistic vision of the world. And there was no seeker more avid than Ken.

What he was seeking one fine day back in 1975 was . . .

Proof that Mars is already supporting a colony of astronauts in a joint venture by the Americans and Russians known as Aries Prime.

Details of this dubious but irrefutable hypothesis were contained in a book entitled *Alternative Three*.

Rumours abound that all copies of this book mysteriously vanished from bookshelves just two days after publication.

But Ken had been reliably informed that a man called Neil was in possession of at least a dozen of them.

He found Neil Oram in a garage near the Gray's Inn Road. He was under a Citroen, mending it. Neil was a tall, broad bear of a man. A shambolic shamanic poet and a seeker to his boots. His West Country accent still prominent despite twenty-five years of travel and adventure, substance appreciation, and pursuits simultaneously spiritual and carnal. Neil never reluctant to expound his unorthodox world view, Ken ever-eager to absorb whatever random information the serendipity of the day lay at his lugholes. Inevitably, they clicked. Neil gave Ken a copy of *Alternative Three*. He also gave him a one-act play. A week later they met in a pub.

The point of a conspiracy theory isn't what you do or don't believe; it's who you *do* believe if you *don't*.

(*Somerset.*) 'At's right; that is profoundly true, Ken. But what did you think of my play?

Would you like a Royal Court sort of answer or a Glasgow Empire sort of answer?

I just want to know what you think.

Well, it's not good.

Oh.

Personally I thought it was complete bollocks.

So you wouldn't want to put it on, then?

Not really, no. Unlike it's terrific author it's puerile and tedious. I have no interest whatsoever in putting on your play.

A'right.

On the other hand, I've firmly made up my mind to put on your life.

My life?

Your *entire life* from the day you left home until the day you met me. And this isn't just some whim. It's an absolute necessity.

So for three weeks the pair of them sat in Ken's garden shed. Neil dictated and Ken typed on an ancient Olivetti. The manuscript they produced was fourteen inches thick, and six copies of it sat in the middle of Ken's living room. He announced that although the play would take twenty-four hours to perform, it would commence at nine-thirty p.m.

Which may sound counter-intuitive, but if we start at nine-thirty we finish at nine-thirty, which even in Scotland still gives us time to get to the pub.

Ken's method of casting was surprising. If not unique.

Yes; when you decide to put a play on you're embarking on a great human enterprise of joyous exploration. And most directors begin that journey looking through *Spotlight*! Is that the best they can do? Flick through bleeding *Spotlight*? I'm looking for actors ready to leap out of their mundane existence on to the highest plane of terpsichordian expression; if they're in *Spotlight* they've already surrendered to the forces of mediocrity. Except Broadbent! He's the only actor in *Spotlight* who actually deserves to be in *Spotlight*. They should just publish a one-page version with Jim in it.

Or they want you to cast someone off the telly.

But if you're on the telly then already you are, by definition; two-dimensional. And it's no good phoning agents and asking them. They're on 15 per cent; they send you an actor and you only get 85 per cent of the bloke. No, no; the best way to cast is to announce what you're up to and see who turns up. Because no one turns up who isn't curious, and so long as you're curious . . . anything's possible. Are you curious?

My mother says I've got a head like an encyclopedia.

Well, that's idiotic. You don't want a head like an encyclopedia; you might as well have a mind like a pile of old newspaper. What you really need is a mind like *origami*.

Had I the gumption I could have been a very young hippy. But the sexual revolution passed me by. I was not hip. I was not tuned in. I was suburban. And I was handed fourteen inches of drama which contained every possible alternative to the life that bred me.

Oram had left home the year I was born. As I mewled, he hitched, as I grew, he went around the world, as I adolesced he communed, as I studied he went transcendental, dianetic, neuro-linguistic, and anywhere his cock or consciousness led him. I struggled home that day with a manuscript that was more than an alternative history, it was in itself an alternative, a deep dark glittering mirror, a portal to other possibilities.

*

First day in Edinburgh we were eating lunch in a small greasy spoon. Ken had just finished his egg and chips and was stood up looking for his hat and paper when a bloke comes in and joins the counter queue. The bloke's holding a rope. On the end of the rope is a goat. (Turns out he brought in the goat because he was thrown out the day before for bringing in his dog.) Ken sits down again.

Well, I think I'll have pudding if there's a goat.

The manageress of the café sees the goat and yells at the bloke in Italian. She chases him out with a rolled-up newspaper. Ken tucks into sponge and custard.

Whatever you do, never let what you decide to do deter you from doing what you actually do. If there's a goat, order a pudding. You get much more pudding that way.

And the strange thing is . . . you start seeing a lot more goats.

Back at the Odeon Russell, as our hero, Phil Masters, has accumulated Oram's manic stares and magic gesticulations.

And I'd been rescued from toilet duty by a sterling fellow called Dick who completed the task with duct tape and hosepipe. Health and Safety duly did an inspection and, disgruntled that the plumbing had been achieved, turned their evil gaze to the lofty ceiling of the fading, flaking Odeon and told us to paint it. So we hired and built a scaffold tower. It didn't reach. We hired a second tower and built it on top of the first.

Now; cinema ceilings are high, and the floor slopes towards the screen end. So the tower had a twelve-inch sway to it. Still, we took two-hour shifts daubing midnight-blue paint on to the ancient plaster. My first shift happily coincided with the first undress rehearsal of the Phil-Masters-shags-his-girlfriend-down-the-bottom-of-the-garden scene. Watched by Ken and most of the company, Russell and petite Paula from Ruislip commenced a committed rehearsal. My poor fortune in being so far from the action was somewhat alleviated by my elevated view. And my relative isolation.

This, seekers, you must remember, was before the days of internet porn, or the DVD, or the VHS. So the opportunity of observing an enthusiastic sex scene from thirty feet above, with no likelihood of anyone looking in my direction, was a gift mightily tempting to unwrap. My enjoyment unfortunately came to a premature climax as the tower lurched forwards eighteen inches and I abandoned the pursuit of pleasure in favour of prolonging my life.

There was to be a lot of sex in *The Warp*. Some of it in the text, much of it in the intepretation. Ken presided over sex scenes like a comedic Caligula, with wide-eyed amusement and unashamed awe. Like a horny-eyebrowed Pan, past his prime but flute aloft, he would orchestrate the youthful enthusiasm of his cast towards the depiction of sexual encounters that were inventive, funny, erotic, and downright rude.

Eithne Hannigan, jazz violinist and robust Irish Catholic, rehearsing with Russell: a long philosophical dialogue about the liberation of the soul and freedom of expression. Eithne is word-perfect, but Ken eventually interupts their Sophoclean discourse.

I think it needs livening up a bit.

Says Ken. 'I couldn't agree more,' says Russell.

Pick up that pad and charcoal. Do a portrait of her.

Russell obeys. They perform half a page or so.

No, it's still a bit dull. Eithne: take your clothes off.

(*Southern Irish.*) What?

If you like.

All of them?

Preferably. I wouldn't think too hard about it if I were you.

So, instead of thinking, Eithne unlaces her Doc Martens. She waves farewell to her jumper, her jeans, and her Kilkenny heritage. Alongside her Ms Selfridge underwear she discards the last vestige of her Catholic upbringing.

Somewhat spellbound, she recommences the scene; but immediately forgets every last one of her lines.

That's absolutely fascinating. That indicates you must have been keeping your lines in your underwear, somewhere.

Well, to be honest wit' you, I'm just a bit embarrassed.

Why?

Well, there's going to be loads of people on the night, so.

Yes, there is; so what you're feeling now is a perfectly natural human response, but one that confines your humanity to the suburbs of knitted sweaters and sensible knickers. It screws you up! Luckily I can sort it for you. Company! Anyone in the stalls or foyer! Eithne's suffering from acute Species Embarrassment. So get down here in front of the stage.

From the four corners of the theatre we assemble and line up between the front row and the apron. Eithne, curled on the sofa, buries her head beneath a cushion.

How do you feel now?

I feel ridiculous.

Well that's because you've got your head under a cushion.

Eithne gets the giggles.

That's your atavistic adjustment mechanism kicking in.

Eithne leaps up and chucks the cushion at him.

So. Do you still feel embarassed?

Well, y . . . No! Fucking no!

Excellent. Russell, take yours off as well, and do the scene again.

Eithne reclines, Russell acts his socks, and everything else, off. There is no doubt amongst any of us that the scene has vastly improved.

Now we're getting somewhere. Russell, if you're drawing this beautiful creature and debating the meaning of life with her, I think you should grow increasingly excited.

Russell grows increasingly excited.

Get animated, Russell.

Russell gets animated.

Sex and art; the meaning of life is sex and art. Express that!

(**Russell**) That's what I'm trying to express.

Well, you're not quite.

So Russell prances and extols, his modest but shameless dick flapping left and stage right, his impassioned husky voice in paroxysms of enthusiastic inflection. But it's not enough.

Paint her with your cock! Rub the charcoal on your cock and paint her with your cock!

Russell blackens his increasingly willing member and paints a somewhat blurred abstract of Eithne, who has entirely succumbed to the giggles.

Don't just laugh at him! He's elevating you. He's transforming you! You're his Venus made flesh.

But Eithne's lines remain lost beneath her discarded clothing; a forgotten part of her previous personality.

If you don't know what to say, have an orgasm!

(**Eithne**) It's alright; I've remembered.

Good. Here's your cushion back; feel free to masturbate. Russell, keep drawing. Excellent.

Excellent indeed. Russell and Eithne sustain the performance for a page and a half until . . .

(**Eithne**) Er, Ken; can we stop a moment? Can I ask something?

What?

(**Eithne**) When we actually perform this, is there going to be music or anything?

Well, not unless you've got a clit that whistles.

A suspended silence, then hysterical laughter. The scene is to end with them shagging. Eithne pulls herself together and has one more question.

(**Eithne**) Ken, can I just ask . . . how are we meant to . . . I mean: are we doing this for real?

And though it comes from a cautious heart there is at the heart of the question a whisper not of *actual* desire, but of the desire . . . for permission. Ken's eyebrows confer with one another.

Well, it depends what you mean by real. Technically you're not obliged to accept Russell's member. But beyond that . . . as real as you fancy, really.

The rehearsal came to an amicable, if feigned climax. We ambled off to paint scenery or eat lunch. Russell and Eithne retire to the dressing room to run lines. And keep it real.

*

That afternoon I was handed a five-page monologue. The loud, indecipherable mutterances of a man at the precarious pinnacle of his first LSD trip.

There was an irony implicit in this, surrounded as I was by a fair number of dope heads, mushroom eaters, trippers, freaks and ketamine enthusiasts; for my consciousness had brought me so little pleasure over the years I had never much fancied expanding it. Beyond a spluttered attempt to inhale a soggy circulating joint, I had never partaken of any mind-altering substance.

And so a fair amount of imagination was going to be called for. I began cautiously. The intensity of the monologue demanded a certain theatricality, but I tempered that with a decent degree of psychological truth. Ken's eyebrows sagged like two minature yaks in the rain.

Is that it?

Well, obviously, there's more to find in it.

More to find in it? You haven't even opened it. You haven't even taken it out of the bleedin' typewriter. There's earth, wind and fire in those words and in your mouth they fizzle out like some soggy fag. You are the plughole of this production; down which all that is great or good is rapidly disappearing. Do it again. I'm going to read the newspaper. If I don't look up you've lost the part. Dick; put that wrench down and watch this; it might be your part.

I do it again. I do it louder. I jump on the table, which is a technique I've seen Ken appreciate on more than one occasion. I consider a degree of nudity which I immediately pretend would be impossible with a script in my hand. Eventually I utilise the face Grotowski makes on the front of the Grotowski book. I finish with a howl of expanded consciousness. And Ken folds his paper.

Well, if you're going to be half-arsed about it I'd better direct you. What sort of actor would you call yourself?

What sort?

What style of acting do you consider your strong point? Brecht? Meyerhold? Reg Varney?

Well, I suppose if I had to . . . well, I was trained in Stanislavsky.

Stanislavsky! Well, why didn't you say so? If it's Stanislavsky you're after we'll do an exercise.

Uh huh?

A sense exercise.

Right.

Hold your hand out. Right. I want you to imagine you've got a ball bearing in your hand. It's about half an inch in diameter and it's quite heavy.

Right.

Have you got it?

Yes. I think so.

Don't think. Imagine.

Right.

Now: imagine it's warming up.

Right.

It's getting hot.

Uh-huh.

It's getting very hot; have you still got it?

Yes. Ow.

Hotter and hotter.

Ow. OW.

Twat. You've got an asbestos glove on.

Right.

It's red hot – can you sense that?

Yup.

It's getting even hotter. It's white-hot now. You've got a white-hot ball bearing in the palm of your hand! Can you feel it?!

Yes.

Good! Now stick it up your arse and do the scene again.

Ken's theatrical taste was relatively simple. He was either stimulated by what he saw, or bored to death.

I think at this point the audience will have lost the will to live. The scene is catastrophically devoid of Italian women with newspapers. Dick! Maria! Get on stage. Roll up those newspapers. Now if he's the least bit dull I want you to pang him! No tiddling little slaps; give him a really good whack.

No one was immune.

John Joyce. Where's John Joyce?

John tumbles eagerly out of a corner, his legs at the double, body braced for potential derision.

(**John**) Yes, Ken?

Last night's postman was very dull.

(**John**) Yes Ken, it was.

All you did was deliver letters.

(**John**) Yup. Well, it says: 'The postman delivers a letter.' That's all it says.

All it says? Have you never heard of *subtext*?

(**John**) Well; the bicycle was my idea.

Well, that's your problem, John. The summation of your imaginative faculties is a bicycle. You are bicycle man. You need inspiring. You've three hours till the half; take this bottle of scotch and down the lot.

(**John**) Well, I try not to drink before a show.

The amount you drink after a show, John, your last drink's just before the half. Tonight we are going to do an experiment. It's entitled 'If a Man Can Stand, Can He Act?'

It's the first time this tried-and-tested acting technique has been empirically examined. In the corner of his dressing room John downs the scotch, with holy conviction that the towering spirits of Burton, Harris and O'Toole will see him safely through it. The experiment is complex. To conclusively prove if a standing man can act, one requires a man who can in fact stand.

When the postman's cue to cometh is imminent, Mitch helps John to the wings and tests another hypothesis: if you put a man on a bicycle and push it, he will surely arrive elsewhere. John arrives centre stage; a bio-mechanical hybrid of man and bicycle, neither upright, neither supporting the other in any way. Untanglement requires a degree of verbal improvisation that is entirely lost on the audience because John has no more control of his tongue than he does of his bike. He searches his pockets for a letter, eventually revealing an imaginary one from his inside jacket. Russell indulges the mime and accepts the invisible letter.

Then the postman, dimly aware he was once criticised for merely delivering one, commences to have a gossip, the subject of which remains unkown to this day. Eventually Russell picks up the bike and throws it into the wings. The postman completes his rendition of 'The Fields of Athenry', and staggers after it.

At the end of the show Ken hands down his judgement:

**The man who is too drunk to stand is not in the least capable
of acting. At least not *as we know it*. He cannot act but he has
absolutely no doubt of his ability to do so, and as a result
performs on *an entirely different plane of being*. It's a tremendous
thing to watch.**

*

At rest, in private thought, Ken's face would be expressionless;
there were times he barely inhabited his face. At such times
he had a clown-like vulnerability, as if the child in him was
wondering why exactly his mother had left him here, to drink
this beer, to walk this dog. But then, a faint twitch of the brows
would indicate that Ken was reconnecting. His eyes would seek
you out. It's disconcerting when a man looks straight at you,
and there were times that Ken would look straight *in* you.

The eyebrows would adjust themselves to the aeronautical trim
required for his mind to take a flight of messianic creativity, or
Machiavellian destruction. No one was immune from the
unexpected Wrath of Ken.

Even St Jim of Broadbent inadvertently raised his ire with an
impersonation of Ken's old pal pig farmer and circus-owner
Mike Hurst, whose indefatigable, mud-spattered optimism
as yet another circus tent collapsed in the mire was lampooned
by Jim.

(*Yorkshire.*) 'Anything's possible if you can put the bugger back
up enough times.'

**You wanker. That, Broadbent, what you just did, is THE
MAGGOT'S VIEW OF THE MIGHTY. Impersonation is the
lowest form of wit. What?!**

*

A few days later, with paint still drying, costumes flying, the
ten-play cycle of *The Warp* is finally under way.

Ha ha!

Russell Denton, as Phil Masters, is about to be in every scene but one. He drinks six eggs and makes his entrance. He has learned seven hundred pages of dialogue. I am failing to retain a page and a half.

Here's the thing; Russell knew every one of his lines, but here's the oddest thing: he knew *every one of yours too.* If you dried he'd just prompt you under his breath. Not only that; if you weren't up to scratch he'd direct you – *ventriloquilly.*

We started off with a promenading audience four-hundred strong. By the early hours there were fewer. At the four a.m. nadir most of the nine or ten punters left were fast asleep somewhere on the set. We were instructed not to wake the audience but to incorporate the unconscious into the action.

Ian Shuttleworth is one of the few human beings to have remained conscious throughout the entire thing. Michael Coveney had a valiant shot at it but fell asleep three times. (He was in the other night and insisted that was an unfair criticism. I referred him to a number of reviews he gave me in the late eighties.)

The rewards for the intrepid were vivid and indelible memories.

Chris Lineham, mad Ozzie . . .

. . . leaping from the circle to the stalls with a lit firework up his arse.

Bunny Reed, polyglot/alcoholic Cambridge scholar . . .

. . . pausing mid-sentence to eat a large Spanish onion.

Neil Cunningham, elite thesbian . . .

. . . depicting a man in a café on an acid trip, decorating his face with a full English breakfast. And shitting a sausage.

It was, however, a long haul. Midway through the second day, the audience had picked up but the company was flagging. Russell and Mya had a long spiritual debate coming up and Ken was fearful it might send everyone to sleep. Mya volunteered to perform it in translucent chiffon with little underneath.

Good idea. And I've got a better one. The ashram debate will no longer take place in the stalls bar. It will take place in a civic arena!

We dutifully marched the entire audience out of the Regal, down the street, into St George's Park and on to the tennis courts, where a previously dispatched Dick had hired a dozen balls and two rackets. We gathered around and watched as Mya, virtually naked, served to Russell, virtually asleep. Between and during points, hitting aces (Russell) and into the pond (Mya), they debated love and longevity, sexual congress, and the yin yan nature of desire. Russell won in three straight sets. And later confessed to me:

That was one of the times I hated Ken. I was exhausted. I was knackered, and here he was marching me to a bleeding playground.

I could have done without it. I nearly threw a racquet at him. Then I see the parky staring at Mya's tits and this bleary-eyed bunch of fools blinking in the sunshine listening to page after page of complete cobblers and someone's selling ice cream and Mya starts giggling and I think: you bastard. You've woken us up. You've *woken us up*.

A few hours later: Phil Masters arriving home from his global travels, meets an amiable part-time brass, goes back to her place, and phones his girlfriend. The brass was being played by Angie; a curvy and disarmingly direct ex-con who had taken up acting in Holloway. Her acting style could be described as defiant.

Russell's actual girlfriend was a fiery Greek called Maria. I was sitting next to her in the dressing room when Angie strode in.

You know I've got to do that blow-job scene with Russell.

(Maria) Oh yes?

I've just nipped in to ask: would you have any objections if I did it for real?

Maria's face illuminates like a paper lantern . . .

(**Maria**) None at all. Go for it!

Word got about. The entire company found a vantage point. I stood next to Ken on a small balcony.

Was this your idea?

Yes; I thought of it last night. But here's the thing: I never shared it with her. You are witnessing the first synchronistically devised blow-job in the history of world theatre.

Depicting a world-weary wanderer was no huge challenge for Russell, who'd been talking, gesturing, and waggling his charcoal cock for nearly a day. Pale and hollow-eyed, he lifts the phone. Angie slips an ice cube into her mouth and slides to her knees.

I have seen on the faces of men looks of ecstatic delight. I have seen on the faces of men looks of sheer exhaustion. I have seen on the faces of men looks of quiet horror.

Never before that evening had I seen all three looks on the face of a man *simultaneously.*

It was from the self-same balcony I observed the hippy body-painting scene. Anyone who wanted to be in the hippy body-painting scene could turn up in it and have their body painted. Or paint a body. I didn't volunteer. I felt, inexplicably, that the naked multi-coloured hippies would wonder *why* I'd volunteered. That I would be poorly judged by the very people so clearly demonstrating their complete lack of judgement. The same with those jeans all those years ago. That sole pair of jeans. The strange conviction that I would walk into a room full of people wearing jeans and they would hold me in contempt for wearing jeans. Which is how the purple jumper man was born. The purple all-over man. And there he still was, stranded on the balcony when for an ounce of courage he could be standing below illuminating Paula's breasts with finger paint, or being painted purple, head to toe, by Mya, forever rainbow-hued.

*

I would sometimes hide in the pub to work on my *Dead Zoo* play now entitled in the hope of further enticing the Royal Court, *Cries from the Mammal House.*

Act One establishes the zoo (Albion) on its uppers, its owners facing financial ruin and their children running feral into mental disorder. In Act Two the animals are slaughtered, the children vanish, and the owner takes his own life. The Royal Court had expressed significant interest.

I would sometimes skip away for hopeful jaunts up Arthur's seat with Mya.

One evening I sidled back in to partake of the strictly vegetarian company meal. Ken was in his cups. I said something. For the life of me I can't remember what, but it was presumably an inane attempt at wit, something contrary to the flow. Enough to separate myself from the proceedings, to grant myself an edge, an above-it-ness. And if there was one form of humour Ken would not tolerate; it was non-celebratory sarcasm.

He veered towards me, and loomed over me. Which is quite a feat for someone four inches shorter than you are.

Where have you been?

Up Arthur's Seat.

You waltz in and out. You don't roll your sleeves up. When are you going to commit yourself to this? I've put five hundred quid of my own money into this and you're obsessed with other stuff, as if there's some other stuff in your life.

Well, there is in fact.

I'll bet it's bollocks.

Well, that's your opinion, I suppose.

You know what your trouble is, Johnson? Apart from your incessant desire to orchestrate misery?

Nnno.

You've got a switch.

His forefinger prodded me on the bone of my sternum.

It's right there. And it's off.

The sternum is a strong but nervous joint. It can be tender. Mine has been tender since that moment. It was a tiny yet brutal assault. It turned my knees to jelly. I thought I would throw up. He staggered off. I stood in a corner of hell and understanding.

The Warp had spat me out.

Interlude

Ken performs the Great Elastic Stunt.

This isn't an interval but if you fancy a pee now's a good time. You've got about three minutes, which gives me time to show something we used to do in the *Roadshow* days. I have here a length of reinforced knicker elastic. Can you examine that, sir? Brings back memories. His glasses have steamed up. And madam – what's your name?

Jenny.

Correct! Can you examine this household brick? Thank you. Now I need a theatrical pioneer. You'll do. Now what I need you to do is stick this in your mouth. Go on. Good. Ladies and gentlemen – The Great Aubergine. Now, I'm going to come amongst you, excuse me . . . (*Etc.*) Now, the Great Aubergine is going to recieve this brick full force in the face. Anyone here like babaganoush? If the people at the front could lean either way. I'm serious. Good. Now when the Aubergine receives the brick you are all going to burst into spontaneous applause.

Are you ready, stage management? Are you ready, ladies and gentlemen? Are *you* ready?

Yes.

Boing, crash, Applause.

Three

The *Hitchhiker's Guide to the Galaxy* had been an enormous and celebrated success on the radio. An enterprising chap called Richard Dunkley decided it deserved a wider audience. Dunkley thought anything could be achieved with a roll of gaffer tape and strong joint.

His instinct as a producer, if something were possible, would be to aim way beyond that for something almost certainly *im*possible. This was the spirit that impressed Ken and saw Dunkley march into the Rainbow Theatre in Finsbury Park and hire it. The logic behind this was impeccable. The *Hitchhiker's Guide* was a romp through space and time hitherto confined to a tiny stage at the ICA. Conversely the Rainbow Theatre was the biggest auditorium in Greater London, thus more closely resembling the universe.

I should have smelt a rat. They were two weeks into rehearsal when Ken called me. I should have sensed the way the wind was blowing. John Joyce wasn't going to be in it. With the wind in that direction I should have smelt that rat.

Ken liked things to be free in every sense of the word. Not because he was mean-spirited, but because he had an increasing body of work behind him that was at its best when produced in penuary.

It's money that fucks it up. You have to account for it. Every time you spend something you owe someone else a *fee* for something else. And people start *moaning*. If he's got a wig, why can't I have my bus fare? As soon as you put money into the equation there's not enough of it.

For *Hitchhiker*, Dunkley had raised a shitload of money. The Russian gangsters looking for UK investment thought they were getting a rock gig.

It was obvious as soon as I entered the desultory church hall that the show was in trouble. Ken's A-team had deserted him for the NT and the telly. Around the edges of the room were a group of aspirant souls who, with a couple of honourable exceptions, were well out of their depth.

I want you to play Zaphod Beeblebrox. It'll suit you. He thinks he's the hero, but he isn't.

Great. Thanks.

Well, in fact I want you to play one half of Zaphod Beeblebrox. This is Doug – he's playing the other half.

A dour Canadian nodded at me; dourly.

Doug's used to being in front, so you'll have to go at the back, and put your head over his shoulder.

(Zaphod Beeblebrox had two heads.)

We haven't got the two-footed boots yet, but when we do it'll be much easier to walk.

(It wasn't.)

Terry, is it?

Hi Doug. How's it going?

You're my third other head so far.

Said Doug's head.

It wasn't an easy part to play. And Doug was at the front. He got all the best lines.

Ken and Richard had gone all out and hired a very illustrious designer, who had gone all out and designed a transforming sculpture of a set to fill the enormous Rainbow stage.

It's complete rubbish. And we can't afford it. Which is a huge advantage, because it's rubbish.

So Dunkley set about designing it himself. There was a scene on the moon. He designed a long crescent-shaped bit of scenery that lay across the forestage from wing to wing.

Richard – what *is* that?

Well, I thought the moon should be made of cheese. So that's the rind.

I don't think it reads.

Well, it's not painted yet. It's going to say 'Edam' on the side.

He designed a spaceship cockpit with flashing controls and a ramp leading up to it. This was Zaphod's domain. Zaphod was being played by two men in one pair of boots. We never once made it up there.

There were lasers that bounced off tiny mirrors in the auditorium and formed a geometric representation of the prow of a space ship. Another lader was rigged to create a cone of light pointing down at the apron through a cloud of stage haze.

Right! Ford and Arthur, stand on the apron. When that laser goes off I want you to jump.

Jump?

Yes, Jump.

Jump where?

Into the orchestra pit.

The what?

It's in front of you. Just step off.

Have you seen the drop, Ken? It's about ten foot.

Well, that's why those mattresses are there! Are you men or mice? Jump!

The lights went out. They jumped.

Je ... sus!

Boing.

Christ.

Ow!

Lights up!

Sure enough, Ford and Arthur were nowhere to be seen. Ken was ecstatic.

Fantastic. That's a first-class example of great theatre craft. The ingenious juxtaposition of a three thousand-watt diode laser and an old mattress!

Any year now they'll be doing it like this at the National.

On the opening night nigh on three thousand people turned up. All of them overweight men between the ages of seventeen and thirty-four.

'Far out in the uncharted backwaters of the unfashionable end of the Western Spiral arm of the Galaxy lies a small unregarded yellow sun.'

Three thousand people raised the roof. The curtain had risen at seven thirty. By ten past eight we had run out of scenery.

The lasers were switched on. But the circle was cantilevered, designed to shift a couple of inches when full. This it had done, and shifted the mirrors with it. The lasers failed to create anything resembling a space ship. But they did shoot out a random matrix of green meanie laser beams, bouncing off hand rails and chandeliers, potentially blinding anyone daft enough to look. It was an audience of sci-fi enthusiasts; most of them risked it.

The whale that falls to earth was a huge inflatable, and it fell from the upper circle. The royal circle got a fine view of it as it flew over their heads. A far better view than those in the stalls, who never saw it coming. Inflatables are not as light as the word might suggest, and after the first performance we were issued with two lawsuits for personal injury, and the whale was grounded.

I'm not a naturally intimate person. I was strapped to the back of a burly surly Canadian, sweat mingling, and thigh rubbing thigh as we struggled to get up the ramp. If we wanted a rest in the wings, he had to sit on my lap.

The curtain came down at twenty past eleven. There may have been as many as a thousand people still in the auditorium. At least a hundred of them applauded. One person cheered. But I think it was Shuttleworth. Thus ironic.

Backstage Ken's face was blanker than I'd ever seen it. The angle of his porkpie was not its familiar jaunty angle.

Well done.

Thanks.

It could probably be shorter.

Yes.

Well done on the ramp.

Thank you.

Nearly got there this time.

Almost.

Terrific.

Ken, in the intergalactic bar scene . . .

What?

Well, I realised we were all standing in front of Michael when he was doing his stuff and they couldn't see Michael.

Right. WELL, YOU DIRECT THE FUCKING SCENE THEN! YOU WANT TO DIRECT IT, GO RIGHT AHEAD. NEVER

MIND YOUR OWN PIDDLING PERFORMANCE, YOU JUST CRITICISE EVERYONE ELSE, WHY DON'T YOU!

My fragile sense of self-worth provided no comeback. I folded. As did the show, mercifully. As did my acting career. I never trod those boards again.

We received the worst notices in the annals of British theatre. It lasted a few weeks, playing to desultory audiences. The gangsters tried to get their money out. Richard didn't want to disappoint them but was firmly cautioned against preferential fraud by a solicitor called Dennis, who was playing a fat alien.

The production was not without its saving grace. Midway through the run Ken strode into the dressing room.

I went to the theatre last night which I rarely do because it's either terrible or terrific and then I'm either bored or jealous. But I went to see Trevor Nunn's production of *Nicholas Nickleby* at the RSC and it was extraordinary. Virtually a new form of epic-politico-psychodramatic-melodrama. So much so I have no idea why the Royal Shakespeare Company is so committed to this endless rote of Shakespeare revivals. If they had any sense they'd wind up the Shakespeare stuff and declare themselves the Royal Dickens Company. In fact, we should declare it for them. We're going to need some headed notepaper. We're going to need typewriters. Who's got a typewriter?

By the end of the matinee the dressing room was a typing pool.

Jane, I want a letter from Trevor to everyone in the RSC informing them of the policy change.

Jim, I want a letter from the board congratulating Trevor on his genius idea.

Terry, you know it all, so I want a letter to everyone in the acting company offering them a role in the inaugural production of *Little Dorrit.*

And no stepping outside the box; I want convincing offers so they'll all accept.

**Maria, a press release. Billington'll be beady but Coveney'll fall
for it.**

We duly composed our epistles and the Royal Dickens
Company was born.

It caused something of a storm in the teacup of theatre world.
Three of the actors accepted their parts in *Little Dorrit*. Ken's
agent, Sally Hope, had been instructed to phone the Aldwych
box office every fifteen minutes to book tickets. Ken called a
special meeting of the pranksters during an interval.

**I've got some good news and some bad news. The bad news is:
we can all be done under the Public Mischief Act of 1872. The
good news is: the posters are ready!**

Thus it was in the dead of night a raiding party circled the
Aldwych Theatre in a small minivan and pasted *Little Dorrit*
posters all over *Henry the Fourth* Parts One and Two.

To his barely disguised annoyance Trevor had to appear on
the telly to reassure the nation he was not dismantling one of
their most persistent theatrical institutions.

'And what would you say to the perpetrator of this hoax. Mr
Nunn?'

I would say nothing. I would throw down the gauntlet.

At which point Ken was revealed, on the line from Liverpool.
Trevor could find no gauntlet to throw, and settled on a tight-
lipped smirk. Ken was unrepentant;

**I'm happy to concede that the whole enterprise was an act of
complete folly! But what could be a finer act than one of utter
folly. And what finer folly than to celebrate the greatest
Dickensian production in the history of world culture. I'm not
denying Shakespeare had his moments but you've been at him
for years now. I think you should give the other chaps a go.**

Four

As in a movie, so in life; the years pass as a *montage* of memory.

I meet him on Borough High Street.

Hello, Ken.

Hello, Genius.

What you doing in this neck of the woods?

I'm at Southwark Crown Court. I'm on jury service.

Really?

Yeah; me and Phil Daniels representing showbusiness. Ten angry men and a double act. We've got to decide if this chap's innocent of guilt or guilty of innocence. My fellow jurors don't think I'm taking it seriously so I've nipped out for a sandwich.

I've never been in a court.

I have. I went through a red light in the *Roadshow* days. I was accused of dangerous driving. Luckily, for the finale, Sylvester was putting the ferrets down his trousers, and we were touring the little bastards, so I said;

'Your honour, as we approached the crossroads the cage fell open and I went through the light with a ferret under my brake pedal.' I pled compassion. He let me off. I was quite looking forward to this week, but it's hard being Henry Fonda. I didn't expect they'd all be so ... guilty.

*

He phones me out of the blue at noon one Wednesday.

What are you doing this afternoon?

Well, I've got a meeting.

Cancel it. I need you to come to the National Theatre.

Um; well I don't think I can really.

It can't be more important than this.

What is it?

I'm doing a workshop. I've got this chap here who needs an audience at two o'clock. He did a great double-take at about eleven, so I taught him the triple-take. Then he tried the quadruple-take. He just did it! He invented the quadruple take! And at two o'clock he *going for the quint*!

*

He does a workshop for the Royal Court entitled 'Dramatic Content and Subsequent Actions'. He arrives with a young woman called Mouse.

He speaks for ten minutes about how an actor's choices should always be dictated by the content of the drama. Then Mouse stands on her head, puts a funnel up her bum and fills it with milk. She executes a neat manouvre on all-fours and sprays the milk out in a ten-foot arc. The would-be playwrights and actors scatter to the four corners of the room.

And that's why content will always dictate your actions.

Says Ken.

*

I convince a producer to cough up a commission and I offer Ken a television series. We sit in his kitchen and talk it through.

'It's about a seeker.' I say. 'It's a comedy. He's a suburban seeker and his wife and daughter have to put up with him. There's a tree at the bottom of the garden that the council want to chop down. And the *you* character has inspired his daughter to be a conservationist, so she lives in the tree.'

Sounds too much like a sitcom to me.

Where's Daisy living?

In the tree at the bottom of the garden.

Well then. Every week, a new obsession. I'm basing this on your play *Couch Potatoes*.

The premise of *Couch Potatoes* is that television is death to the soul. If you try to put the terrific stuff that's not on television on the television it won't be terrific, it'll just be more stuff.

Not for you then?

No, no. I suppose I'll give it a go. I shall write a television series the sole objective of which will be to make everyone who watches it switch the television off. Which seems to me to be more or less what the BBC *do*.

Is Daisy happy up the tree?

Yeah. I said she could leave school if I home-schooled her. I'm setting her a series of educational tasks. Living in the tree's her first semester.

What's her next one?

Punch and Judy. I've given her the swazzle. As soon as she works out what it is I'll give her the puppets.

Does she have to do an exam or anything?

No.

Do you think she'll stay the course?

Yes. I told her to learn *Hamlet*. She said she'd rather learn *The Warp*. So she's learning *The Warp*.

So will you write the series?

Yes. I shall call it; *The Off Switch*.

My sternum tingled. We gave him six thousand quid for a pilot episode. We never saw a page of it.

*

But Daisy learns *The Warp* and performs it in a Portakabin in Hounslow one weekend. Then she mounts her own full-scale production . . .

And gets knocked up by the Irish character man.

Daisy's baby appears as the baby Daisy played in Ken's original.

One weekend, exasperated with her father's technophobia, Daisy gave Ken a substantial sum of money and sent him out to buy a computer. He returned home with an African Grey parrot.

*

The utterances you least believe . . .

Ken summons the renowned actor, teacher and philosopher Jeremy Stockwell to get the first bus to his house by the River Lee. They discuss improvisation, teleportation, divorce and Japan. At the end of the meeting Ken hands Jeremy a carrier bag full of Arabic newspaper.

Take this.

Said Ken.

I think you might need it.

Ken *puts his hat on.*

One evening I too am summoned. I take my friendly buxom friend Hetty because I think they might just hit it off. Warren Mitchel is there. The parrot's having a quiet night. The dogs are caged because the dogs are dangerous because Ken once met a man on the marshes who trained dangerous dogs and Ken was so impressed he bought them. Ken leads us down into the basement to share his latest enthusiasm.

I've met a local psychic who's on speaking terms with the late Sir Laurence Olivier. I enquired of Larry who, in his opinion, is the greatest living actor? That's indisputable, replied Sir Laurence. It's Jackie Chan.

Ken shares with us his mission to watch Jackie Chan's life work; he has fifty three VHSs. Luckily he knows where the best bits are. There are some younger people at the gathering who had only heard tell of *The Warp*. Ken shows them a few scenes from a blurry old recording of one of the ICA performances.

This was a show we did, well, it was some time ago. We didn't have much money, which helped a lot, I think. There were great people in it, because in those days the arseholes tended to drift away. Whereas now I seem to attract them. Terry here was in it. He drifted away but not in the way an arsehole drifts. He was never an arsehole.

Oh, I think I was, you know.

No, no. You occasionally looked like an arsehole but that's because you were talking through it at the time.

You had to look like one or you'd have been facing the wrong way for your chosen mode of communication.

Well, that's nice of you to say so.

Credit where it's due. It was a long time ago we put this play on. Way back when. Back when there was hope, I suppose. Back when I had hope.

A thousand words a day fly in one ear and out the other but on the occasional day a few words settle, to live in your ear, and alter forever the way you hear all the words to come.

Back when I had hope, I suppose.

I drove Hetty home. She and Ken never got together. I often think I should have driven off and left her there.

Time passes. And then there is the time beyond hope that must be passed, until it becomes the past.

*

Ken's death was not expected. Ken died . . . unexpectedly.

The dogs had been released and fed. His medication by the bed, well-ordered, and all of it accounted for. His Last Will and Testament, and other documents of importance only to the living, were tidily set out on his desk. Daisy found him.

Five

I'm buried in Epping Forest. Apparently you can be.

So we gathered in the forest for Ken's End-of-the-Road Show. It sounds like a fairy tale, but it was slightly creepy.

I think it might be Daisy's revenge for those three months in the tree.

I stood apart. Which is mostly what I've always done. Watching is my way of joining in.

I looked at our faces, grown old. Such an expressive collection of faces, yet this morning, this mourning, so devoid of expression. We had all buried relatives, but this seemed like our first true funeral. The first intimation of our own mortality, how close it can come, how close it will come.

John Joyce looked especially hollowed; his face an empty vessel, as if it had forgotten every last thing that life had taught it. He was the most eloquent of us all, though he didn't speak a word. His eyes invited mine, but the light in them was faulty, and the darkness beyond the flicker was fathomless.

Mya and I hugged, and found brief solace in remembrance of the Liverpool days we had sailed her big brass bed aloft in the junkyard attic of our temporary lives, holding on for dear life.

Tom Conti accompanies his daughter. My regard for Tom Conti takes flight.

The chapel in the forest is very suburban and very small. Family and close friends fill it. The rest of us on folding chairs beyond the doors, sitting in the chill open air, listening to the service through modest loudspeakers.

We finger the order of service; a modest slip of folded A4, like a theatre programme for those shows we did when we were young. A modest, fond page of ephemera, destined to hang for a few years under a fridge magnet, and to pang the heart when you go for the Edam.

It begins as it continues: strangely. From the modest speakers, a familiar voice.

Good morning, seekers. It has come to my attention that FUNERAL is an anagram. It's an anagram of REAL FUN.

And in each and every heart a flutter. That the showman in him was audacious, mad and cruel enough to gather us for a sixty-seventh birthday in the woods; funereally disguised. Momentarily we share the hope he lost, but no; even for Ken that would be a caper too far.

Warren Mitchell, comic firebrand quenched in loss, tries to wrestle the grim hand of his own mortality from his bent old shoulders by telling inappropriate jokes. His wreath is woven from their shared roots of bawdy old East End innuendo; he tosses it like a quoit, and misses the peg.

Impossibly young children read unbearable poignant poems.

Dave and Jane and Jim reminisce. The tall tales, the songs, the anecdotes, ring hollow. Specious moments from the past, set out like dry seashells on a suburban mantelpiece.

Young man Sam from *The School of Night* rushes into the chapel and wrestles the lid off the coffin. Daisy escorts him outside as he cries:

(*Sam.*) I don't want him to be dead!!!

As he runs away into the woods, the disgraced Chris Langham, recently released, is heard to mutter: 'Well, this is the best gig I've been to in ten months.'

Tom Conti takes charge and stands glowering at the door. My regard for Tom Conti wavers. Mya shouts into the forest;

(*Mya.*) We love you, Sam!

The ghost of a lion is the least settled of ghosts.

We circled the grave amidst the trees while Irving played sax and we threw handfuls of earth on to a cardboard coffin.

Epilogue

My desire to orchestrate misery has never left me and in my darker hours I still search for the note he never left. According to Stockwell . . .

Ken had been experimenting with the phenomenon of out-of-body travel, and had reported finding himself, on more than one occasion, atop the wardrobe looking down.

Perhaps, Jeremy ponders . . .

He got out and couldn't get back in.

There is a woody fragrance in the air, a vetiver note, the flipside to the scent of roses on awakening. A sense that he knew his time had come.

In his sixty-seventh year he had outlived the alcoholic highs that once drove him to creative extravagence or maudlin vituperation, outpaced the health issues that sent him striding over the marshes, training those impossible dogs, and had waved a no doubt regretful farewell to the charm and magic that bedded him those divine violinists, those glorious ventriloquists. For if a man is beyond pleasure, what more should he seek? Ken was a champion of seekers, but the reaper wears the crown.

*

Listen. If you listen you can hear the ghost roar.

*

I finished my *Dead Zoo* play. The Royal Court put it on.

It was terrific.

It wasn't my best. But Ben Benison taught Tim Roth to be a praying mantis.

And he's been one ever since.

Act One still set in the bankrupt zoo-slash-Albion. In the last act the Animal Kindom still gets slaughtered.

But between Acts One and Three an inspired Act Two . . . an Odyssey to Mauritius, meetings with remarkable folk and a valiant attempt to save from extinction the Pink Pidgeon. The play is dedicated to me!

Without whom . . . Russell's in the *Guinness Book of Records* for playing the longest part in the history of. Seven times *Hamlet*. I cast him in an Ayckbourn at Bolton. He played a man with a bad back who couldn't get out of bed. He was very funny. And he never worked again. He became a school caretaker. He nurtured the gardens, and the kids.

John Joyce, a few weeks after Ken's death, in his familiar way, like an enlightening gem of an addendum at the foot of a page, quietly died.

His admiration and fondness for Ken never in doubt now here, in a cleft heart, was the irrefutable evidence of love.

Daisy became a playwright.

And writes a play about Robert Anton Wilson in which I appear. I would have been proud to play myself but unfortunately I was dead by then. But genius playwright Terry Johnson; who, incidentally, was one of my chaps, tells me that in his opinion she's really *really* good at it.

If wishes are a promise to the past then I wish many things.

I wish I'd done the body painting scene.

I wish I'd done EST, and LSD in Liverpool with Sir Jim of Broadbent.

I wish I'd kissed Mya in the drizzle up on Arthur's Seat. I wish Mya . . . was just one woman.

I wish I'd put Ken in a play.

I've seen you: rummaging about in that head of yours, trying to work out how other people think. Imagining yourself in other colours, searching for a pleasing hue of body paint. And in *Cries from the Doo Dah* the hero arrives for the epilogue carrying a

large crate, and in the crate alive and well, no less, a dodo. Think of me as the only drug you ever took! Voodoo me do, whenever you please.

And I do. If it's a delicate acting moment I remember Ray McAnnaly in his cups: 'Acting now; well, that's just the art of changing the look in the other feller's eye.'

But for everything else it's Ken I conjure. For that inverted film star distracted by narcissism, for that inexperienced dreamboat struggling with her confidence, for that angry man trying not to be angry, for all those real moments when real acting is really the concern, then it's Ken to the fore.

There's a hole in my forehead; and out he comes; I unleash the Vaudeville beast and howl the words that go right to the heart of the matter; piercing that diffidence, inflating that confidence, chucking a brick in that narcissist's pond. With that bit of Ken between my teeth then I'm complete.

I almost told you to be a ventriloquist but I'm glad I didn't; I think I made the right call with Nina. If you nudge the tiller at the right moment they don't notice at the time, but a few years later they're in a different hemisphere.

I no longer wear purple; indeed I have a pathological aversion to it. But I feel it on me. My hair will never again brush my shoulders, I razor it to invisibility, but unknown to the world, I still part it on the side.

You've got a switch there, and it's off.

I can feel the finger on my sternum still. For in eleven seconds and seven words I was given damn near half my personality. And seekers, it was the finest half. He saw it in me and he pinned it and he named it, and he told me where the switch was.

It's hard to know what to believe, sometimes. We find it harder and harder until we're in danger of believing in nothing. But the alternative to believing nothing is to BELIEVE in EVERYTHING. There's only one word in the English language which approximates the true nature of the Universe and that word is 'OTHER'! And every little once in a while THE OTHER WILL MANIFEST and it's good to be around at those times, because if you've the courage THERE MAY BE SOMETHING UP FOR GRABS!

I find it hard to keep the switch on. The off position is my gravity. It's my nature to be earthed to the point of entropy. But I always know where to find it, and as I grow older, I reach for it more often. And Ken, for some small part of every day; I find it, and I flip it, and I glimmer with a little of the light you shed.

Thank you. That's probably the end then.

Yes.

Well, I think it went quite well. Well done.

Thank you.

Mind you; you could do with a stronger finish. What I think that you should do now, if you want this evening to be truly memorable, is take all your clothes off and paint yourself purple.

End.

For a complete listing of Bloomsbury
Methuen Drama titles, visit:
www.bloomsbury.com/drama

Follow us on Twitter and keep up to date
with our news and publications
@MethuenDrama